D1465792

An introduction to
Risk Management

An introduction to
Risk Management

Second edition

NEIL CROCKFORD, BA, FCII, MIL, MIInf.Sc.

WOODHEAD-FAULKNER · CAMBRIDGE

Published by Woodhead-Faulkner Limited
Fitzwilliam House, 32 Trumpington Street, Cambridge CB2 1QY, England,
and 27 South Main Street, Wolfeboro, NH 03894-2069, USA.

First published 1980
Second impression 1982
Second edition 1986

British Library Cataloguing in Publication Data
Crockford, Neil
   An introduction to risk management.
   2nd ed.
   1. Risk management
   I. Title
   658.4'03   HD61

   ISBN 0-85941-332-2

Designed by Ron Jones
Typeset by Hands Fotoset, Leicester
Printed in Great Britain by St Edmundsbury Press, Bury St Edmunds, Suffolk

Contents

Preface

There is nothing very complicated about risk management. Yet, para-doxically, that is why it needs explanation. To a large extent it can be summed up as common sense codified, but "common sense" is usually only what seems an obvious line of thought or action to the person using the expression. One man's common sense is another's novel concept, while it is heresy to a third, and nonsense to a fourth. Applied to risk management, which, as a technique designed to help a company stay in business, has to be broad enough to apply to all its activities, the danger is that common sense will become restricted to what seems obvious to the particular specialist one is dealing with at the time.

A whole range of measures for tackling risk will be necessary, and most of them will probably appear to be common sense to someone. It is not enough, however, to announce that the object is to manage risk, and leave everyone in the company to use common sense about how it is done. The result would only be a hotch-potch of plans, some overlapping, some conflicting. Some types of risk would be managed effectively, while others were ignored because they were no one's specific responsibility. Common sense is not enough; the element of co-ordination is vital.

Without that, the essence of risk management would be contained in the closing lines of William McGonagall's triumphantly bad poem *The Tay Bridge Disaster*:

> For the stronger we our houses do build
> The less chance we have of being killed.

That is common sense all right. Surely no one could disagree with such a blinding glimpse of the obvious. But consider the proposition. A stronger house will certainly reduce the risk of it collapsing on one's head, but perhaps that extra strength has been gained at the cost of making it more difficult to escape if the house catches fire, and it does nothing for one's safety away from the house.

Managing risk means dealing with it in all its aspects, not just those which happen to be most familiar, and uniting many different skills in a common effort. The need for co-ordination is, I think, something that has been insufficiently stressed in much of the literature of risk management. Too often one facet of the subject is treated as if it were the whole. Some insurance men write as if risk management were another name for self-insurance. Some safety experts imply that it is solely a matter of accident prevention. There are statisticians for whom it all revolves around probability distributions. Each specialist sees risk management in terms of his own special interest, with the result that the message is fragmented among a number of "sects", each claiming to preach it all.

The outsider may find it hard to distinguish between orthodoxy and heresy, and his confusion is not lessened by the fact that not only is much that is written about risk management produced by specialists, but it also tends to be written for other specialists. There is very little for the general reader. That is why the articles which have now become this book were written. The intention was to provide the non-specialist – business man, student, or indeed anyone curious about what risk management is – with a general introduction to the subject which would indicate its breadth and underline the importance of a co-ordinated approach to the handling of risk in all its variety.

A book like this can never be one man's work alone. The ideas in it have, of course, been influenced by the many discussions I have been privileged to have over the years with risk management enthusiasts of all kinds: practising risk managers, insurers, brokers, loss prevention specialists, consultants, academics and many others, in the United States as well as Europe. I have learned much, too, from the management and staff of the companies in which I have put some of these ideas into practice. All of these are, in a sense, fellow-contributors to this book. Only any errors are unequivocally my own.

My special thanks are, however, due to those who have helped with advice on and suggestions for specific chapters, and in particular to Hugh Spencer, Jim Bannister and Linda Simpson. I should also like to thank the Editor of *Foresight – The Journal of Risk Management,* in whose pages these articles first appeared, for permission to reproduce them in this form.

Neil Crockford

Preface to the Second Edition

The basic principles of risk management are unchanging, but because it is a response to the problems of risk posed by an environment which is constantly being modified, the relative importance of those problems and the detail of the solutions available will not always be the same.

We are now emerging from a period in which the ready availability of insurance at low rates and on generous conditions has concentrated attention upon that particular method of treating risk. As we enter a phase in which a seller's market is developing in insurance, there is once again a real incentive to deploy all the skills of risk management. It is therefore an appropriate time to present this revised edition which takes account of the main developments affecting risk management in the years since this book was first written.

One welcome development has been the much greater acceptance of risk management ideas, particularly in the insurance world. It is especially gratifying to see that the principles of risk management, once widely seen as inimical to insurance, are now summarised in the Chartered Insurance Institute's examination textbook, *Elements of Insurance,* as the starting point for newcomers to the industry. More than that, the CII has introduced risk management itself as an examination subject for Fellowship students, rightly treating it as a management subject, rather than as a purely insurance subject.

In revising this book, therefore, I have introduced some new material with the syllabus of that examination in mind in order to increase its value to students, without departing from my original intention of providing a simple introductory guide to risk management, and without seeking to duplicate the specialist literature of its component parts.

Other changes have been made to reflect the effect that risk management itself has had. Captive insurance companies, for example, have attracted the attention of tax authorities both in the USA and in this country, and modifications to the law have borne heavily upon captive companies formed primarily as a means of avoiding or deferring tax, rather than as valid risk financing vehicles which can be justified as an integral part of a full risk management programme. The chapter on captives has thus been updated in the light of the new tax environment and the consequent emphasis upon group and association captives.

The opportunity has been taken to add new material, such as the chapter on contingency and emergency planning. This deserves separate treatment as, in one form or another, it underlies all loss control. Other changes have been made wherever necessary in order to clarify the points made, to cite new or more appropriate examples, and, in one or two cases, to correct errors of fact.

Neil Crockford
April 1986

1. Introduction

This is the age of the expert. The quantity of human knowledge has accumulated at such a rate that greater and greater specialisation has become both a necessity and the pride of the experts. This pride has all too often led to the specialist erecting a fence around his own small property in the world of ideas; but fences that are too high to let the neighbours see in can also have the disadvantage of being too high for the householder to see what his neighbours are doing.

There comes a point, therefore, when it becomes essential for someone to take a wider view and to point out that all these carefully separated properties are in fact part of a single community. Risk management, or rather the term "risk management" (for I shall be at pains in what follows to distinguish between the comparative newness of the name and the long history of the practice), is the result of one such wider view developed by some far-seeing insurance managers in industry and academics in the field of risk and insurance, who took the necessary step back from their particular specialisation to realise that their work and that of many others, in security, fire prevention, health and safety at work, economics, law, management and a wider range of disciplines, all had something in common. Each was concerned, to a greater or lesser extent, with risk – with identifying it, evaluating it, minimising it, or dealing with its consequences.

Risk management, therefore, sought from the start to bring together again an essentially simple concept which had become complicated out of all recognition by its fragmentation into separate disciplines, the practitioners of which each had a few interlocking parts of the jigsaw and believed they had the whole picture.

Intellectual exclusiveness had played its part in this fragmentation, but to a large extent it was implicit in the development of human society. For primitive Man, there was a clear link between the correct appraisal and treatment of the risks that threatened him and his survival. Broadly speaking, this awareness of the balance between risk and security in all he did was apparent to the individual until comparatively recent times. Industrialisation, the division of labour and the advance of science and

1

technology have, however, made it increasingly difficult to identify the risks threatening his personal safety or his economic well-being. Risks, of which he may be completely unaware, are imposed upon him and upon all members of society.

Corporations have become larger and more complex, and machines and industrial processes too complicated to be understood by those operating them. The link between a man's attitude to risk and his actions on one hand, and the physical and economic consequences to him on the other, is not now so clear to see. Not only are risk factors affected by an increasing number of variables outside the individual's control, but also the number of these variables has encouraged the emergence of specialists in all the different aspects of risk handling. Each of these has tended to create his own terminology, consequently adding communication difficulties to all the other problems.

While this complexity was developing (and to some extent as a counter to it), the simple, easily understood and widely effective mechanism of insurance was making great progress as a risk treating device. So successful has it been that it is now for many industrial organisations the first and only answer to the problem of risk.

For such organisations, risk identification becomes a matter of selecting from the wares the insurer is prepared to offer; risk evaluation means fixing sums insured in a way to suit the insurers, or buying limits of liability on the basis of what suits the budget or what the insurance market will offer; risk reduction is limited to that for which there is a premium rebate. To say that a purely insurance approach is often an expensive and incomplete answer to the problem of risk is not to detract from the value of insurance. It has served industry well and is likely to have its place in the most advanced risk management programme. It is, however, essential, for a full understanding of what risk management is, and what it seeks to do, to end the identification of "risk" with "insurance".

Looked at in the new perspective of risk management, all the various disciplines touching upon risk can be seen as contributing towards an overall technique for tackling risk and its problems. In industry, for example, some companies are beginning to realise that their safety specialists and their insurance specialists should be working in concert, whereas historically they have kept well apart from each other, acknowledging each other's existence with suspicion, if at all, and reporting along different management chains.

Risk management as an integrated procedure is still much more often talked about than practised, but there are encouraging signs that co-operation is replacing competition between some at least of those responsible for the practical implementation of various aspects of risk treatment. Similarly, in the financial sphere, there is growing recognition that conventional insurance is not the only, nor always the most appropriate, way of providing for loss.

The new understanding that risk does not respect administrative demarcation lines has necessarily created new techniques. There is little that is new about the contents of most of these techniques, for in many cases they have long been used by one or other of the various specialists in the fragmented world of risk treatment. The novelty lies in their application to the field of risk as a whole and in the combination of different measures drawn from disciplines which in the past have had little to do with each other.

This book is about the new risk management philosophy. That means it will touch upon insurance, self-insurance programmes, loss prevention, fire protection, security, accident prevention, legal liabilities, pollution and many other subjects, each of which has its own specialist literature. It will not try to duplicate that literature. Quite simply the aim will be to look at risk wherever it occurs, and to show how the philosophy of risk management can help in solving the problems that risk creates.

Risk management stands at the place where all the many specialisations which I have mentioned meet. It must not, however, seek to elevate itself into a new specialisation, for this would be merely to repeat the errors of the past. Risk management must always be a linking function, ready to learn from the expertise of specialists and to communicate that expertise to other fields where it may have fresh application. Above all, it must preserve its view of risk as a whole and resist any attempt that may be made to treat any particular aspect of risk as a special case calling for entirely different treatment.

Academic writing on risk management has so far tended to try to erect such barriers, notably between areas of risk where there is a possibility of either a profit or a loss, which they have labelled "speculative" risk, and those other areas where there is only the possibility of a loss, which they have called "pure" risk. Only the latter, it is claimed, is the province of risk management. Neat though the division is in theory, in a practical business situation it becomes extremely difficult to determine exactly where any such dividing line runs. To attempt to subdivide risk is open to the objection that it effectively equates risk management with the job description of the individual in a company who holds the title of "Risk Manager". This title is normally given to a man who is required to concern himself only, in general, with those risks which have traditionally been financed by insurance. This is administratively convenient, since this part of the world of risk alone will give him a wide enough area of responsibility to keep him fully occupied. One must beware of thinking, however, that there is a fundamental difference between the philosophy that should be applied to the risks within his province and those other risks to which the company is exposed. In both cases the same process of risk identification, evaluation and treatment must be carried out. Risk management is notoriously difficult to define adequately, but it can be considered as simply the application to the particular problems of risk of the normal processes of management decision-making, which are as follows:

3

(*a*) defining the problem;
(*b*) evaluating possible solutions;
(*c*) selecting and implementing the optimal solution;
(*d*) monitoring the performance of the solution.

Risk management is thus a special case of management, but all forms of management will contain some degree of risk management.

Viewed in this light, it is clear that individuals and companies have always managed risk to some extent. The technique of risk management seeks to apply known methods of dealing with the problem of risk in a more effective and more ordered form and to devise new or improved methods of minimising or financing loss. In the next two chapters I will discuss the character of risk, dealing first with the various types of risk and then examining how it can vary in its severity and frequency.

2. Types of risk

Vulnerabilities

In a static world, where the possibility of change did not exist, "risk" would be a superfluous word, or at most it would express a metaphysical concept. For a risk to become a loss some change in existing circumstances is essential and thus without change risk becomes meaningless. Change is, however, all around us, and, since no one can be sure about the form that change will take, we are surrounded by uncertainty.

Without uncertainty, the world as we know it could not exist, and yet it is that same uncertainty which presents the major threats to the continuance of individuals and organisations. However well the factors governing possible change that are within one's control are managed, no one can gain mastery over all the other external factors of change. As a result, man lives surrounded by threats – threats of injury or death, of financial loss or of failure to achieve aims and ambitions. For a business, uncertainty will threaten future earnings and cash flow, assets owned now or acquired in the future, the uninterrupted flow of services or goods and, in the extreme case, the continued existence of the business. Uncertainty cannot be entirely eliminated, and wherever there is uncertainty there is risk. As Peter F. Drucker puts it: "To try to eliminate risk in business enterprise is futile. Risk is inherent to the commitment of present resources to future expectations. Indeed, economic progress can be defined as the ability to take greater risks. The attempt to eliminate risks, even the attempt to minimise them, can only make them irrational and unbearable. It can only result in that greatest risk of all: rigidity."[*]

It is important to appreciate that there is a positive side to uncertainty as well as the negative one. Just as a loss can be incurred through accepting, or being exposed to, a risk (either recognised or unrecognised), so also the acceptance of the right risk may lead to gain. The writers on risk management who have divided risk up into "speculative" risk and "pure" risk, placing in the first category those risks which have the possibility of advantage, recognise that all risks are not threats and

---

[*]*Management Tasks, Responsibilities and Practice*, Heinemann, 1973.

that all risks are not therefore to be avoided. In concentrating on the "pure" risks, however, as being proper subjects for risk management treatment, they reflect the popular conception of risk as something undesirable. Most of the dictionary definitions of risk, for example, relate it to hazard or threat. This is understandable, since good fortune does not usually present anyone with serious problems.

To concentrate one's risk management thinking on the "pure" risks only is, however, to deny that risk management procedures have anything to do with deciding whether or not a particular "speculative" risk should be accepted. It is good risk management to minimise the effects of a pure risk, but so it is to maximise the chances of a speculative risk producing a positive rather than a negative result.

Risk can never be totally eliminated. The probability of a particular type of loss may be reduced to zero, but this can only be done by changing some of the circumstances surrounding the risk. As soon as circumstances change, a new set of risks is created, which may be either greater or less than the risk that has been eliminated. This should not be taken as a reason for doing nothing about risk. Any action that can economically be taken to reduce risk is worth taking. What it does mean is that the process of risk management must be a continuing one. To identify and deal with the risks threatening a business is but one aspect of the process, not the process itself. The risks created by the risk management process must also be analysed and dealt with, and there must be a continuing review of the modification to risks brought about by changing external circumstances.

Risk expresses itself in a company in financial terms: in the variability or potential variability in its assets, earnings, cash flow or in the services it exists to supply. The following are some of the wide range of uncertainties which threaten a business. As will be seen, the possibility of loss is not limited to the obvious direct consequences, nor need the results of these risks necessarily be wholly adverse.

Natural perils

Damage by fire, windstorm, flood or other natural catastrophe is probably the most immediately apparent threat to a company's material property, just as the interruption that may result is the chief threat to its earnings. But it is not impossible that a loss of some vital stocks could lead to scarcity, to increased prices for surviving stocks and for those produced when operations are resumed, and therefore to an increase in earnings.

Loss of personnel

Death or injury to employees may involve the obvious direct costs of compensation for the injury, or insurance premiums to transfer that cost, time lost at the time an accident occurs, and possibly fines for breaches of legislation. There will, however, be indirect costs as well – the time that has to be spent in investigating the accident and in compiling the necessary reports and attending any subsequent legal proceedings, the losses of production which stem from any property damage associated with the accident, the time spent by staff who may not have been directly involved in discussing the accident, and any industrial relations problems that the apparent lack of safety may cause. Then there is the cost of recruiting or training someone else to carry out the injured employee's task. This could be considerable where special skills or knowledge are involved. Loss of a key employee, for example in a research-based company, could have a disastrous effect on the business.

Labour risk

Even in the absence of accidents, employment involves risks for a company. The availability of suitable labour may be fundamental to its success. Vulnerability to the effects of staff dissatisfaction may also be crucial and if measures are introduced which might increase unrest, it may call for fine judgement to balance the advantage to be gained from the measures against the possibility of a lengthy withdrawal of labour or co-operation.

Liability risks

Every business faces the possibility that a single event could involve it in crippling liabilities to third parties. For many companies these days, particularly those supplying products to the USA, this is one of the chief threats to be faced. The risk of liability is, in any event, worse for being capricious. It bears no relation to the size of the company, or the value of what it owns, and once the chain of events that leads to a liability begins, it is largely fortuitous whether the loss that results will be trivial or serious.

The time scale of liability risks is increasing all the time. Limitation periods have become much less rigidly enforced and liability may now be incurred as a result of circumstances which happened many years ago, and even where the possibility of injury or damage was unsuspected or discounted at that time. The effect of long-standing liabilities on asbestos firms in recent years has provided a dramatic example.

Technical risk

The industrial scene is rapidly being transformed from one where change happened at a pace which gave time for adjustment to it, time to adapt methods of action and thought to it and time to handle it, to one where change occurs at a pace which makes ordered and adequate preparation for it much more difficult. The time span between a research discovery being made and its incorporation into standard technology is shortening all the time, and there is an increasing risk that the performance targets set for a new plant may not, or even cannot, be attained. The introduction of a new process carries risks which could have either positive or negative results. It could produce all the benefits expected from it. On the other hand, if it were late coming on stream, or if full-scale production threw up unexpected problems, the result might be a serious loss.

7

Marketing risk

The launch of any new product involves the risk that, however well the market has been researched, customers may reject it. The proportion of new products which survive to gain a significant market share is very small. Even if it becomes established, there is always the possibility that a change in needs, attitudes, taste or fashion may render it obsolete. Equally, fashion may revive an apparently superseded product, as the vogue for blue jeans did for non-fast indigo dyes.

Political and social risks

Until recent years, political risk could be defined as the risk of nationalisation, sequestration or other government intervention, but it is now used to include acts of terrorism and politically motivated hi-jacking and kidnapping. Political action need not, however, be as extreme as that to introduce variability into a company's fortunes. The introduction or abolition of grants or local incentives to industry may have either a favourable or an adverse effect on its business, as may changes in legislation affecting its production methods, its products or its customers. Such changes may reflect a development in general public opinion or be the result of a campaign by a sectional pressure group which may be able to influence the way a company's business is carried on, even in advance of legislation. Such non-governmental influences constitute social risks which often resemble, and are intertwined with, political risks proper.

Environmental risks

The risk of harming the world about it and those who live there has been a steadily increasing one for industry over the past century. The constraints upon permissible contamination of air, water and land are becoming more severe all the time, and legal penalties for pollution can be very costly to a company. This is a particular form of social risk which is arousing special public concern, as the arguments of the already strong environmental lobby find popular support in the wake of disasters such as that at Bhopal.

The need for security

In the pyramid which Maslow* used to illustrate his theory of the hierarchy of need, the individual's need for security occupies an important place, only simple physiological needs for food, warmth and shelter being shown as more basic.

The need for individual security is carried over into business life in a number of ways. First, the individual must feel secure in his job, which in most cases is the means by which he is able to satisfy the more basic needs

---

Motivation and Personality, Harper, New York, 1954.

8

of food, warmth and shelter. On top of this there will be a desire among management to avoid the risk of criticism from those to whom, or for whom, they are responsible, if their actions can be shown to have adversely affected the success of the business.

So far as fortuitous and external risks are concerned, most companies simplify the problem of how to cope with threats to their assets or earnings into a choice of whether or not to insure. The alternatives are rarely weighed in any objective manner; more often than not a decision to insure is taken because insurance of some part of the risk is compulsory, because the risk has always been insured, or because to insure is normal practice, and a decision not to insure would have to be explained, and perhaps justified. Other risks may be left uninsured for reasons which have more to do with a subjective feeling that the premium asked is too high than with the probable severity or frequency of the risk.

In this area of risk, the tendency to use, and to over-use, insurance has been increased, apart from the cheapness of insurance in recent years, by the fact that the purchase of insurance has often been looked upon as a necessary but undoubtedly tedious business, undeserving of the attention of top management. It has often been delegated to an insurance manager of relatively low status within the company, or left as just another of the many administrative jobs which the company secretary has to handle. Not only has risk not received the top-level attention it deserves, but risk treatment has thus been left to a group of people who, if it were possible to draw up a personality profile of them, would probably prove in most cases to be more risk averse than the average.

This may explain why there are so few true risk managers in industry despite the growing interest in risk management as a subject. It may also explain why, in the field of "speculative" risks (traditionally the field of the entrepreneur who must, almost by definition, have more of the gambler in his make-up), the problem of uncertainty is met with much more imaginative solutions. There we find a much wider range of management techniques, which make it possible to look at and treat risk on its merits and not simply to think of it as something to be avoided at all costs. As Peter Drucker says: "The main goal of a management science must be to enable business to take the right risk. Indeed, it must be to enable business to take greater risks – by providing knowledge and understanding of alternative risks and alternative expectations; by identifying the resources and efforts needed for desired results; by mobilising energy for contribution; and by measuring results against expectations, thereby providing means for early correction of wrong or inadequate decisions."* It is the application of this philosophy to the field of pure risk that what has come to be known as risk management sets out to achieve.

Management Tasks, Responsibilities and Practice.

Management approach to speculative risks

It is interesting to compare the way in which a company approaches a speculative risk decision with the way in which it deals with a pure risk decision of a similar size.

The speculative risk will be undertaken with a view to profit, and will therefore be perceived as forming part of the function the company exists to carry out. For that reason, it will engage the attention of senior management. If it is to be financed externally, the bank or financial institution involved will be concerned to see that the prospects for the project have been properly evaluated.

A financial case will have to be made for the project, the amount and rate of return will have to be estimated, and the present value of that return calculated. The risks of failure must be calculated and the means of circumventing them examined. The maximum tolerable loss will have to be determined and a time-scale set within which the project must produce its results. In effect, a detailed risk analysis, involving identification, evaluation and loss reduction proposals, will be carried out and there will be a "go/no go" decision point when the project will be approved or rejected, usually at a high level within the company.

When it comes to pure risk, however, the picture is very different. In the vast majority of companies, insurance is still seen as the normal solution and insurance will be bought without using any of the analytical techniques which would be applied to a speculative risk. The "go/no go" decision is much less likely to be affected by pure risk considerations than by speculative risk ones. One disadvantage of this is that the option of avoiding pure risks is often removed, and opportunities for reducing their probability or severity may be limited by decisions already taken on speculative risk grounds. Certainly insurance is much less likely to be subjected to a rigorous cost-benefit analysis than any other expenditure of comparable size.

The result is that insurance is bought without asking the simple questions which it would often be standard practice to ask about the speculative risks facing the company:

(a) What are the risks?
(b) What is the probability of loss from them?
(c) How much are the losses likely to cost?
(d) What might the losses be if the worst happened?

It is only by asking and obtaining the best possible answers to these questions that one can determine whether insurance is necessary or optional, or whether the particular insurance contract that is offered is worth buying.

3. The severity and frequency of risk

To generalise, it is possible to divide losses into four types, with differing characteristics of frequency, severity and predictability, as shown in Fig. 3.1.

Type of loss	Frequency	Severity	Predictability
Trivial	*Very high*	*Very low*	*Very high*
Small	*High*	*Low*	*Reasonable within 1 year*
Medium	*Low*	*Medium*	*Reasonable within say 10 years*
Large	*Very low*	*High*	*Minimal*

Fig. 3.1   *Loss characteristics*

Trivial losses are to be expected in any organisation and can be met from normal operating budgets without inconvenience. Some loss prevention may be possible, but it may be uneconomic except for those types of risk which are normally acceptable, but which might have much more serious effects if circumstances were to change slightly.

Small losses, too, present little problem, unless their frequency becomes so high that their aggregate effect approaches that of a single medium loss. Fortunately, small losses can often be reduced by fairly simple loss control measures. Distribution of these losses over the year may vary in response to external factors. A bad spell of winter weather will increase accidental damage to motor vehicles, for example, and this may occur before Christmas in one year and after in another, while it may be absent altogether in some years. There will thus be some fluctuation, but it will usually be possible to make a reasonably accurate prediction of the probable overall cost.

11

The medium losses would not cause the business serious concern if they happened at regular intervals, for then their cost could be expressed as an annual amount and provision made for it. But this is not the case and predictability is the variable which causes concern, because one can never tell whether this is the year in which such a loss will happen and if so how many medium losses there will be. In the longer term predictability is reasonably good but because of the period that must elapse before this is achieved, a business is likely to need short-term help in dealing with this type of loss.

The large loss presents the most serious problem. A loss of this kind happens very rarely, but if it did occur, it could be catastrophic for the business. The difficulty arises from the fact that no one can foretell when such a loss will occur, or even if it will occur at all. It is in solving the problem of the larger loss that insurance has its justification for large organisations today.

The relative frequency of losses in these four classes can be shown as a pyramid (Fig. 3.2). The distribution this illustrates holds good both:

(a) *Geographically,* for losses occurring at one location or in one company or industry over a relatively short period; or

(b) *Chronologically,* for all losses over an extended period.

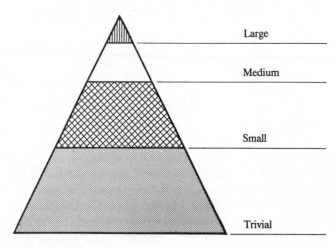

Fig. 3.2 *Relative frequency of losses*

Applying the characteristics set out in Fig. 3.1 to this distribution, it can be seen that frequency and severity of loss are inversely proportional, so that, as the one rises, the other falls (Fig. 3.3).

Insurance rating

Although an individual may need insurance protection against all but the very smallest losses, companies have higher thresholds of retainable loss

12

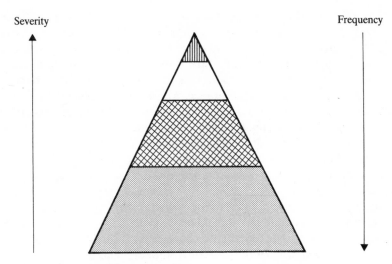

Severity

Frequency

Fig. 3.3   *Severity and frequency of loss*

and one might expect insurers to concentrate on offering them cover against more severe risks only. Insurers' wider spread of loss statistics should enable them to forecast the occurrence of such losses more accurately than a company relying on the limited statistics at its disposal could do, and they would be spared the administrative expense of settling the many small claims.

This, after all, is how insurers themselves buy insurance. They retain the small losses which present no threat to their financial stability and buy reinsurance for the more serious risks. They have historically, however, been reluctant to sell insurance in this way, preferring to issue policies which include cover against small, and sometimes even trivial, risks as well as against the large ones for which protection is really needed. "Excesses" or "deductibles", by which the insured bears the cost of smaller risks, have often been rewarded with smaller premium reductions than they deserve.

The essence of insurance from the buyer's point of view is that it substitutes a small certain loss (the premium) for an uncertain and possibly much larger loss. It thus provides at least a partial solution to the problem of uncertainty. It does this, however, in a very crude way and if the buyer is to be sure that the insurance solution is the best in economic terms, he must be certain that the insurance is exactly tailored to his needs, in terms both of insured values and of the types of loss covered. He must also set up a monitoring system to make sure that he is kept informed of new and changing values at risk, and also to see that the operating activities of his company are such that the policy conditions are complied with. It need hardly be said that this is a very difficult task.

The rating mechanisms used by insurers are very imprecise, and are of only limited help in assessing the true possibility of loss. There are two basic methods – class rating and experience rating – which are used for most types of insurance. Class rating applies the total loss experience to the total sums exposed in a group of similar risks to produce an average loss ratio, which, after addition of the insurer's expenses, profit element and other corrections, becomes the class rate. Experience rating departs from the original concept of insurance as a device for paying the losses of the few from the contributions of the many, by considering the record of the individual insured only. Future premiums are calculated from the past actual losses with the addition of expenses, profit and other corrections. This form of rating is applied to such insurances as those of large motor vehicle fleets, and most reinsurance treaties are, at least in part, experience-rated.

Neither of these methods of rating is wholly objective, because there must always be an element of individual judgement in deciding the extent to which the past is to be taken as a guide to future experience. The optimism or pessimism of the underwriter, or any bias in his judgement, may lead to rates which are higher or lower than the risk in fact warrants. The fluctuations in market capacity for industrial and commercial insurances also have a cyclical effect upon rating. When there are many insurers interested in covering a particular class of risk, over-supply may drive rates down to uneconomic levels. When underwriting losses result, rates may shoot up until they are far too high in objective terms.

Recent years have shown such a cycle in operation. High interest rates encouraged new entries into the reinsurance market because of the availability of premiums for investment. The supply of reinsurance was further increased by the trend for large industrial and commercial companies to form 'captive' insurance subsidiaries (see Chapter 9) which often transacted reinsurance. Increasing supply drove reinsurance rates down, thus reducing the need for direct insurers to underwrite so selectively, since it was easy for them to pass the undesirable portion of the risks they accepted on to the reinsurance market.

Direct insurers themselves were inclined to put the emphasis on obtaining premium income to invest. Premium rates tumbled and restrictive conditions on policies were eased as insurers fought to retain their market share. This had its consequences for risk management, as risk managers found insurance being offered at rates which could only lead to an underwriting loss for the insurer. The exercise of purchasing skills in the insurance market thus became economically more effective in the short term than the application of all the skills of risk management.

Inevitably, there came a change. Interest rates fell, the claims, although slower to arrive than the premiums, at last began to reach the reinsurers and many of the new entrants to the market found reinsurance becoming unprofitable and withdrew from, or were forced out of, the business. Reduced reinsurance capacity and the realisation that investment profits would no longer cancel out underwriting losses forced direct insurers back to prudent underwriting and to charging premiums which reflected the risk. Rates thus began to rise sharply, making proper risk management once again a priority for the insured, to counter the tendency by insurers to apply an over-correction and to set rates which were, objectively, too high.

4. The systematic identification of risk

It is self-evident that no orderly plan for the treatment of risks can be put into effect until it is known exactly what the risks are. The need for identification will, however, vary according to the particular part of the risk management process that is the main concern of the person doing the identification.

Those concerned with the practical aspects of loss control will, for example, need to identify in minute detail the risks presented by particular locations, processes or machines if they are to design or install suitable preventive devices. Those whose concern is the financing of risk, particularly by insurance, will, however, tend to identify risks in much broader categories, because their concern is to establish boundaries of cover for classes of risk, whether they have been identified in detail or not. Both sides have developed a wide range of tools and methods to suit their own purposes, but in each case the approach is too limited for adaptation to the needs of an overall risk management investigation.

Components of risk

Any risk is made up of four components, which we may classify as:

1. *Threats* – the broad range of forces which could produce an adverse result;
2. *Resources* – the assets, people or earnings which could be affected by the threats, i.e. the things on which the operation depends for continuity;
3. *Modifying factors* – those particular features, internal or external to the resources, which tend to increase or reduce the probability of the threat becoming a reality, or the severity of the consequences if it does;
4. *Consequences* – the manner in which, or the extent to which, the threat manifests its effects upon the resources.

In their consideration of risk, insurance people concentrate on consequences. They tend to think of risks in terms such as material damage risks, personal accident risks, liability risks, interruption risks etc., classifying them according to the effect produced. Classification of this kind is, however, of limited use in seeking to identify threats if the aim is to prevent them producing the consequences.

Because of their much more detailed approach, those concerned with loss control tend to limit their enquiry to specific types of threat. Their specialisation may effectively narrow their perception of risk, so that the only threats that are considered are those to which they already have an answer. Threats which are more remote may easily fall within the gaps between specialisations, and thus not be identified at all, if the approach is from loss control. Where, however, there is good liaison between the areas of specialisation, loss control can be the basis of a very efficient system of risk management. The example of the US space programme comes immediately to mind.

Commercial enterprises, however, can neither afford expenditure comparable with that of a space programme, nor are their operations generally surrounded by the dramatic dangers of the unknown. What they need is an overall approach which will provide guidelines to the sequence in which the identification programme should be carried out and also prompt enquiry about risk which might otherwise be over-looked. It must ensure that the search ranges over all the possibilities, or at least that all the possibilities are acknowledged. Essentially it must focus the mind on what it is really looking for – risk in all its guises. The jargon of specialists and the plethora of definitions of risk can lead to confusion, because one man's exact definition of risk, for his particular purposes, may well exclude whole areas of what another man calls risk. The definition of risk used by a mathematician in calculating probabilities is different from that which is appropriate for a person concerned with the need to reduce damage.

Risk and everyday experience

Most people would find the accepted definitions of risk and uncertainty incomprehensible, but everyone has the capacity to identify risk. A mother seeing her child about to step off the pavement of a busy road doesn't think to herself: "Here is a situation involving the chance of variability from the expected outcome." She simply thinks: "He may be run over."

This same example, however, shows the limitations of intuitive identification of risk. The obvious risk has been identified immediately, but there are countless other threats to the child's safety which it is most unlikely the mother would ever consider. The wall alongside the pave-ment might collapse on him, some toxic or corrosive material might suddenly escape from that tanker which appears to be passing at a safe distance, there might be an earthquake, or the child might be struck by something falling from an aircraft high overhead. The list of possibilities can be extended as long as you like.

In practice, as far as personal risks are concerned, most people take some steps to manage the obvious risks, but tend to assume that the more remote have a zero probability. This contrasts with the common attitude to chances of gain. Most people filling in a football pools coupon do so because they feel they have an outside chance of winning a fortune, yet most of them at the same time will regard their chances of being the victim of a statistically much more probable accident as too remote to be contemplated.

Charting risk

Clearly this concentration on the obvious risk and rejection of the more remote is not good enough for an ordered programme of risk management, but even the fullest programme must begin with the obvious risks and work outwards from them. To begin with, the search for risk must be reduced to its simplest terms and the single question that must be asked is: "What can go wrong?" The field of enquiry implied by that question is a wide one, and if from that field we take a simple, but broad concept, that of threats to operations, we can begin to analyse the risk in a logical way in terms of the four components of risk listed above.

Under each of the headings, "Threats", "Resources", "Modifying factors", and "Consequences", one can set down as full a range of possibilities as one requires. Under "Threats", for example, such things as fire, pollution, breakage, etc., may be listed; under "Resources", all the men, materials, plant, etc., that the operation depends on; under "Modifying factors", points of siting, construction, market standing, etc.; and under "Consequences", the way in which the resources will be affected, in terms of damage, injury, liability, interruption, etc.

Once the columns have been completed it is possible to arrange the various items in the different columns alongside one another and consider how they interrelate. One can consider the resources in turn and relate each threat to them, or one can start with each threat and consider which of the resources come within its range and which of the modifying factors increase or decrease the risk. Alternatively, one can start from the other end and look at each of the consequences in turn, considering which of the resources are subject to them, by which modifying factors they are affected, and which of the threats would be necessary to produce those particular consequences in each case.

This method is capable of producing either very broad or very detailed pictures of risk, according to what is needed, but it has to be based upon an on-the-spot examination of operations. It is possible to sit at a desk and draw up a theoretical risk picture based on supposition and generalisation about an industry, but this will be a very inaccurate guide to the risks which threaten a particular business. In risk identification, there is no substitute for going out to see what is done, how it is done, where it is done, by whom it is done and what is used to do it, or for asking questions of the people involved in the day-to-day operations, who are often the only people who know what goes on in fact, as distinct from what is presumed to go on.

They may, however, have no incentive or channel to pass on their awareness of risk to someone with the authority to have something done about it. Only by going to see for himself can the risk manager gauge the extent to which departures from standard procedures are authorised or condoned, or how temporary arrangements (and temporary arrangements can easily become permanent) can affect normal operations.

Using this first-hand knowledge of the operations, the listing of the different components of risk provides a very useful and adaptable tool. Under "Resources", for example, one might consider a building as a whole, or break it down into its component floors, sections, or process areas. A project might be considered as a whole from the initial idea to completion, or it might be broken down into successive stages. A machine might be thought of as forming part of all the plant and machinery in a factory or as a single item, or again as a combination of many different components and the threats to each component analysed.

This technique is therefore useful both to the insurance man, thinking in terms of consequences and broad categories, and to the loss prevention engineer, thinking of particular threats in extreme detail. Through it, each can obtain a fuller risk picture and one which does not have the limitations of his speciality built into it. It can ensure that all the risk factors are identified, although the degree of detail about each factor will vary for each person in the risk management process and will depend upon how much detail he needs to carry out his particular risk treatment function.

In practical risk management, however, it will not be found necessary to set down all the listings under the various headings on paper, unless this method of charting risks is adopted as a formal record. Provided the various factors are borne in mind as the location is visited, or the project is discussed in detail, the key risks can be identified without difficulty. In order to go through the possible range of threats systematically some form of check list will probably be found useful.

Check lists

Many forms of classification have been suggested as the basis of useful check lists, so there is no lack of choice. The soundest plan is to adopt those lists which appear to be most relevant to the business under consideration, to use them and to modify them from experience until they become second nature. Above all, one should never fall into the trap of thinking that one has finally arrived at the definitive check list. However neatly it has been adapted, it will always be capable of further adaptation. The following are some of the approaches which might be used.

Categories of "Resources"

This would list the various types of buildings, plant, materials, products and other property owned, or the property of others for which the business is responsible, or with which it may be involved. People, both employees and non-employees, involved in or affected by the business would also be included. Using this check list it will be possible to spot the threats which exist to each of these categories and the consequences which would follow from the operation of each particular threat.

Categories of "Consequences"

Here one would list the various situations of disadvantage in which a business might find itself: loss of or damage to assets, loss of income, liabilities incurred, interruption of operations, etc. Using these as a starting point, one can look to see whether each of the resources one is considering could be affected by such a consequence and which threat would be necessary to produce it.

Categories of "Threat"

This would begin with the broad classifications of types of threat: natural forces, human error, deliberate damage, progressive deterioration. The inclusion of the last category is important, as it is all too easy to think only of external or suddenly operating threats and to overlook the fact that operations can be interrupted just as severely because a piece of equipment is worn out or because it, or an organisational process, has ceased to operate as efficiently as it should. These broad categories of threat can be broken down to include the specific threats which might endanger the resources that one is considering and from this the likely consequences can be projected.

Other possible check lists follow a chain of events, in order to identify the risks associated with each stage. Among these are the following.

Flow charts

Constructing diagrams to show the flow of materials, services and information within a company, a department, a building or a process can be very helpful in identifying potential vulnerabilities. Significant concentrations of resources and possible production bottlenecks are often made more apparent by schematic representation. The dependence of different parts of the operation on one another can also be revealed.

The diagrams should preferably be annotated with the values at risk at each stage of the operation, since the point of maximum concentration of materials may not necessarily represent the organisation's maximum potential exposure to loss.

Energy chain

The chain of events followed may be expressed in more fundamental terms than would usually be found in a flow chart. For example, any operation can be thought of as involving a redistribution of energy, and it would be possible to construct a check list which considered the build-up and release of energy in the operation, how each could go wrong, what might be affected in consequence, and what the result would be for the company.

Other check lists can be compiled from existing information sources within the organisation and outside.

Written sources

The emphasis here is on identifying potential "consequences", which can then be related back to the resources which would be involved and the threats which would produce the consequences. Such a check list would include the various types of record available within a company, such as:

(a) financial and accounting records;
(b) fixed assets registers;
(c) maps, plans, photographs and descriptions of premises, plants and processes, etc.;
(d) loss records – statistical and financial – and descriptions of particular incidents;
(e) procedural manuals;
(f) contracts and leases;
(g) conditions of sale and purchase;
(h) promotional material describing the organisation;
(i) insurance policies – for example, a study of the exclusions from a liability policy may suggest threats which might otherwise be overlooked;
(j) competitors' literature;
(k) trade journals and other published information about the industry;
(l) the wide variety of other records available.

Responsibilities within the organisation

This form of check list follows the organisation chart of the company and, by listing the responsibilities of each official, helps to identify the threats to the smooth running of his particular part of the organisation, the resources under his control and the consequences which it is his responsibility to avoid or to put right.

Check lists can play a useful part in prompting the sort of questions that must be asked in identifying risk, but they must never be looked upon as giving all the possible variations on the question "What happens if . . .?", which can usefully be asked. Above all, it is important not to use a single check list on its own. The possibility of a major omission will be greatly reduced if it is cross-checked by use of another check list which uses a different starting point. It must be emphasised again, however, that check lists and other desk research must be supplemented, wherever possible, by site visits.

Using the risk chart

The formal statement of "Threats", "Resources", "Modifying factors" and "Consequences" can perform two useful functions once a risk management programme has been instituted.

First, it provides a convenient means of recording information on which that plan has been based, so that it may be up-dated from time to time by local management. If they are required to study the chart and set out, in the same form, any changes in circumstances which have taken place since the chart was drawn up, the information is more likely to be accurate and complete, because a logical framework for it will have been provided in a form which will be readily understood.

Secondly, the chart can be used as an effective training aid for management, since it can quickly demonstrate the many-sided nature of risk, the multiplicity of risks which can surround any single operation and the variety of ways in which those risks can be reduced or controlled. In using it for this purpose, however, care should always be taken to avoid giving the impression that it is the job of line management to identify risk only, and for the risk manager, or any other single person, to do something about it. Identification is only a preliminary to risk control, which must also be seen to be the responsibility of line management. Risk management, if it is to be effective, must be seen to be part of management and not as a form of magic practised by remote control by one particular official.

5. Risk measurement

Hand in hand with the identification process goes that of risk measurement. One cannot pose the question, "What happens if . . .?", without prompting the further questions: "How serious would it be?" and "How likely is it to happen?" Risk has thus to be measured in two dimensions – those of potential severity and probability. Severity is the easier of the two to estimate in most cases, but neither can ever be more than estimates, because both involve looking into the future. The only guide to the future is what has happened in the past, as modified by factors observable in the present or which may develop later. The information on which measurement is based will therefore also be incomplete, but this should not be used as an excuse for not trying to make the best possible estimate.

Fortunately, some help can be derived from the relationship between severity and frequency mentioned in Chapter 3. Once an approximate value has been obtained for the potential severity of a risk, it is possible to make an assumption about its probability. As we have seen, the greater the severity, the smaller the probability is likely to be. This is not, of course, an absolute rule, for there may well be risks where loss prevention is so bad that a major loss is more likely to happen than not, but thorough risk identification should reveal anomalies of this kind.

Measuring severity

So far, risk has only been classified as "large", "medium", "small" or "trivial", but these terms are not exact enough to be useful in practical risk management. First, it must be recognised that each of these will represent a different level of risk for organisations of different sizes. What is a trivial risk to a multinational concern may be a major one to a corner shop.

Secondly, the aim of risk measurement is to locate the risk on the pyramid of severity,* so that it is possible to make decisions about whether the risk is an acceptable one and, if not, what action can be taken

---

*See Fig. 3.3 on page 13.

to avoid, transfer or reduce it. For each company, the boundaries between each category of risk will be set at specific financial levels, in order that the more accurately its severity can be measured, the more certain one can be about the category into which the risk falls. Similarly, accurate measurement of the severity after risk reduction measures have been applied will reveal whether or not the object of pushing the risk down into a lower category has been achieved.

Thirdly, the case for risk management expenditure, as for any other in business, must be argued in financial terms. To talk of a "large" risk is insufficient, because the term is vague and subjective, and to do so deserves to be met with the question: "How large, exactly?"

The measurement of severity for risk management purposes should not be confused with the exercise of fixing values for insurance purposes. That is done within the context of the cover provided by the policy, and what is uninsurable must be omitted. Many indirect costs will not therefore be included in the insurance calculation, but they form part of the loss which the organisation would have to face if the risk produced its effects, and thus cannot be omitted from the risk measurement calculation.

Sums insured in property insurance are based on the replacement cost. For risk management purposes, the cost that has to be assessed is not only that of replacing the damaged property, but also that of all the time and materials which are lost and all the expenses which will be incurred in overcoming the interruption to the flow of earnings caused by the loss. For insurance purposes, one can think separately of material damage and consequential loss. For risk measurement purposes, one must combine these and include costs which neither policy would cover.

Risks to property

For property such as raw materials, work in progress, finished stock and cash, measuring the probable cost of loss will not be too difficult, because replacement, which involves a readily ascertainable cost, will usually be the most efficient post-loss strategy. The total cost will then be the cost of replacement plus the cost of any delay in obtaining replacements.

With capital assets, the problem is more difficult because, in order to know what the loss would be, one needs to know what the company would do if it were suddenly deprived of their use. Unless this has been considered in advance, one has to assume that the asset would be replaced, but this might not be the quickest or the most effective way of getting back to full profitability. The opportunity might be taken to make some operational changes which would improve efficiency.

If, for example, a soft drink firm lost its bottling plant for a popular drink which sold in large quantities, but with a low profit margin, it might have a number of options. It could simply replace the line, it could have the bottling done by another firm on contract, it could cease to do the bottling itself, but set up a franchise arrangement with a number of local bottlers around the country, or it could phase the product out and replace it with, say, a vitamin-rich drink with a healthy image which offered a much higher rate of return.

From the risk management point of view, the cost of the risk of losing the bottling plant would differ according to which of these options were chosen. Although the loss in replacement terms might be a major risk for the company, the opportunities it would give might be such that a true risk management assessment would rate it a minor risk. Contingency planning for major losses, which will be discussed in Chapter 11, is thus essential for good risk measurement.

In considering losses of property, one cannot look at particular items in isolation. One must always consider what else might be lost or damaged at the same time. It is not enough to know, for instance, that an explosion would cause considerable damage. It will be necessary to know, for risk management purposes, just how much damage is to be expected, what will be affected, and how much of that would belong to the company and how much to others. It is possible to calculate the over-pressures which could be generated by an explosion at any of the probable locations in and around the site, and how far the effects could be expected to spread. By plotting the various. over-pressure zones on a plan of the area, it is possible to estimate the extent of damage that would be caused and, based on the type of property involved, the likely maximum cost.

Comparable techniques can be devised for a whole range of threats, and using them can save a company from being in the embarrassing situation of having to say after a disaster: "We had no idea it could be so bad." On the other hand, accurate measurement may show that the effects of a threat have been over-estimated, and that what was intuitively thought of as a catastrophic risk was in fact one which, although still serious, was capable of management by the company.

Risks to employees

In addition to the cost of compensation, or of premiums paid to insure against it, injuries to employees will involve many indirect costs, which must be taken into account when measuring the risk. There often will be a considerable amount of time lost at the time of the accident and, subsequently, while the circumstances are reported and investigated, and when criminal or civil proceedings arise. Although production may continue during these events, some employees, particularly members of management, are bound to be diverted from their normal activities, and this cannot be done without incurring a cost.

The accident may lower morale and productivity in the company, or it may induce a tendency to over-caution among employees in the short term. If an accident reveals serious safety shortcomings, strikes or restricted working may be among the costs of the accident. Whether or not the employer was to blame for the occurrence of the accident, the injured employee will have to be replaced, either temporarily or permanently. This may mean reorganising the duties of other employees, or recruiting and training a replacement, all of which will involve costs. If it is a key employee whose services have been lost, finding a replacement may be very expensive, and there may be a substantial loss of business in the meantime.

Senior management is not exempt from injury. More than one company has suffered considerable financial loss because several members of its board have been killed while travelling together. In a small company or partnership, the loss of goodwill or of the entrepreneurial drive could mean the end of the business.

These indirect costs are very difficult to quantify, but awareness of their existence will enable a contingency amount to be added to the foreseeable direct costs. It may also help in the identification of particularly high risks, and give clues to suitable loss reduction measures.

Interruption risks

Here the important questions to be asked concern the nature and purpose of the organisation – does it exist to make a profit or is its main aim the continued supply of a service? How important is it to the organisation to get back to normal quickly?

At one extreme will be the organisation which provides a vital service – a specialised hospital, say, or a water authority, where it is essential to restore the service as quickly as possible, even at an "uneconomic" cost. At the other extreme is a company which, because of the lack of alternative suppliers or because of the nature of its contracts for supply, can suspend operations until the effects of the loss event have been rectified and then restart operations without serious financial penalty.

Most organisations will be somewhere between these extremes. They will need to estimate the additional expenditure they would have to incur for temporary resources or alternative methods of operation (which again will be simpler if a proper contingency planning exercise has been carried out), plus the net loss of income attributable to the loss during and after the period of interruption.

Financial risks

In the field of pure risks, the most important are likely to be the risks of theft or fraud and credit risks. In measuring exposure to the risk of dishonesty, one must try to estimate the maximum amount that any person, or group of persons acting in collusion, could steal before being detected. Large cash losses may attract most attention, but it should not be forgotten that a long-running stock fraud may be more costly than a spectacular robbery.

Computer fraud has come into prominence in recent years, although there is rarely anything new in the nature of the frauds perpetrated. The use of the computer system, not only to commit the theft, but also to conceal it, can make detection much more difficult, and so it is wise to be pessimistic when estimating the amount which possibly might be stolen in this way. If one is looking at the past as a guide to the future in measuring this type of risk, one should always remember that the really successful frauds are the undetected ones which do not appear in the records.

In measuring credit risks, one at least has a maximum figure to work from, which will be the maximum amount owed to the organisation at any one time. To this must be added the value of any stock made to the special order of particular clients which would be awaiting delivery, and for which there would be no other ready market. Given that maximum figure, it will be a matter of judgement as to what percentage of it represents the true extent of the risk.

Risks of liability

Liability risks present the greatest difficulty in being measured because liability is not a constant, but is modified as the attitudes of society change. There has been a rapid increase in the extent of liabilities, particularly those of manufacturers and the professions and there may be many years' interval between the action which gives rise to a liability and the notification of a claim.

Another problem is that each liability has a unique cost, which is, in the last resort, dependent upon the opinion of the court that hears the case. Added to this will be any consequent costs of investigating and administering the claim, and those of making any changes in operational methods or products which may be necessary to avoid a repetition of the event giving rise to liability. The latter will be the amount in the sum over which there will be the greatest degree of doubt.

By keeping oneself informed of trends in liability and of the amounts currently being awarded by courts in the areas in which the company trades, and by making the best assumptions possible about the number of persons who might be injured and the type and amount of property which might be damaged, it should be feasible to make a broad estimate of the extent of liability. Since transfer by insurance is normally the preferred method of handling liability risk, this will help in deciding suitable policy limits. The consequential loss to the company cannot, however, be insured and this potentially disastrous risk must never be left out of the calculation.

Aggregation of risk

Risks have so far been treated in this chapter as if their effects were felt separately. In reality, of course, a single incident can give rise to damage to property, injury to employees and liabilities to others. It is necessary, therefore, to analyse potential loss-producing events and to find the aggregate of all the costs which may flow from them, remembering that the ultimate cost may be out of all proportion to the apparent severity of the initiating cause. It will never be possible to predict such a total cost with complete accuracy, and the best procedure is to calculate a range of potential severities. The worst case must not be omitted, but one should not become hypnotised by it. It should be balanced by a prediction which represents the most favourable case, and one between the two extremes which constitutes the best guess of the likely cost. All these predictions must, of course, be updated as circumstances change.

It also should never be forgotten that the occurrence of pure risks is likely to be random and that the unpredictability will increase with the severity of the risk. There may be, say, one chance in five hundred of a large fire loss in any one year, but there could still be two in two years or even two in one month. The measurements discussed so far in this chapter relate only to the cost per occurrence. It will be necessary to consider how many such losses the company could stand in one year, and its spread of risk, before deciding what position on the pyramid of severity to allot to the risk in question, and taking the appropriate action to reduce it.

Measuring probability

The only evidence on which estimations of the probability of future events can be made is what has happened in the past, therefore the more relevant data of past losses that is available for analysis, the more confident one can be about the probability of future events. That is not to say that history will repeat itself. No entirely accurate assessment of probability can be made except in retrospect, when the probability will always be seen to have been either 0 (it did not happen) or 1 (it happened). Absolute certainty that a future event will happen is impossible and it is difficult to allot a zero probability to any event that does not contravene natural laws. Estimating probabilities, therefore, means allotting a value between 0 and 1 to the event under consideration.

Some knowledge of the science of probability and probability distribution is thus of great value to the risk manager. It should be a matter of concern that so little use is made of it in risk management practice. The depth of knowledge required is not great and is available in simple textbooks of statistics for business, but there is a reluctance among risk managers to accept that numeracy is part of their required qualities. Fortunately, it is not necessary to be able to construct and test distributions or to understand the formulae involved to make some use of probability theory. Obviously, the better the risk manager's own knowledge of the subject, the greater can be its contribution to his decisions. Many risk managers could, however, improve their risk measurement by having a simple computer program prepared to analyse past loss data using the most appropriate distribution so as to give estimates of probabilities of each level of severity.

Even this second-hand application of probability theory will emphasise the need for the fullest records of past losses to be kept, and the convenience of grouping this data into classes of different size which may be equated with particular levels on the company's individual pyramid of severity.

Of the various probability distributions which may be used, the risk manager is most likely to find the Poisson distribution helpful, as it can be used to estimate the probability of a particular number of events, such as the number of fires of a certain degree of severity, occurring. If one estimates the expected number of such events on the basis of past data, one can, by using this distribution, obtain values for the probability of any number of the events occurring.

If, say, one has calculated in this way that the total probability of zero, one, two and three fires is 0.39, then one can use the fact that the probability of all outcomes must together equal *1* (or certainty) to deduce that the probability of more than three fires occurring is 0.61. One can also decide the probable maximum number of fires by observing at what number of occurrences the probability becomes virtually zero.

Once probabilities have been allotted to future events, whether by the use of probability distributions or intuitively, they can be used to improve decision making in risk management. Consider the case of a risk manager who has made three predictions about the cost of loss if each of four courses of action is taken. These are shown in Fig. 5.1. With no information about probability, one can only assume that all three cases are equally likely, applying what is called the criterion of insufficient reason.

Course of action	Cost of loss (£)		
	Best case	Intermediate case	Worst case
1	40,000	60,000	80,000
2	50,000	60,000	70,000
3	35,000	50,000	85,000
4	40,000	70,000	125,000

Fig. 5.1 *Risk management alternatives*

The probability in each case will thus be one third, and multiplying each cost by this probability will give an expected cost for each option, as follows:

Option 1	$40,000 \times \frac{1}{3} + 60,000 \times \frac{1}{3} + 80,000 \times \frac{1}{3} = 60,000$
Option 2	$50,000 \times \frac{1}{3} + 60,000 \times \frac{1}{3} + 70,000 \times \frac{1}{3} = 60,000$
Option 3	$35,000 \times \frac{1}{3} + 50,000 \times \frac{1}{3} + 85,000 \times \frac{1}{3} = 56,667$
Option 4	$40,000 \times \frac{1}{3} + 70,000 \times \frac{1}{3} + 125,000 \times \frac{1}{3} = 78,333$

In this case, Option 3 would appear to be the best, although its advantage over Options 1 and 2 is not large enough for it to be an unchallenged choice.

However, the risk manager may not feel that all the cases are equally likely, or that they should be so treated. The attitude of his company may show risk aversion, or it may encourage the taking of a certain amount of risk, and this thinking might colour the decisions to be taken.

The risk averse company might feel it wise to assume that the worst would always happen, and so would choose Option 2 as it gave the best result in those circumstances. Similarly, the risk preferring company might assume that the best case would always happen and so would select Option 3.

These are, however, the extremes of optimism and pessimism. The risk manager might try to place his company between these two extremes by calculating an expected cost from the figures for the best and worst cases only, allotting probabilities to each which express his degree of optimism. Thus a moderate pessimist might use 0.6 for the worst case and 0.4 for the best case.

If, however, some measure of estimated probability has been obtained for the various outcomes, this can be used to obtain an objective expected cost. If, for example, the estimated probability of the best case is 0.2, that of the intermediate case is 0.5 and that of the worst case is 0.3 (assuming, for simplicity's sake, that no other outcomes are possible), the calculation will be as follows:

Option 1 $\quad 40,000 \times 0.2 + 60,000 \times 0.5 + \quad 80,000 \times 0.3 = 62,000$
Option 2 $\quad 50,000 \times 0.2 + 60,000 \times 0.5 + \quad 70,000 \times 0.3 = 61,000$
Option 3 $\quad 35,000 \times 0.2 + 50,000 \times 0.5 + \quad 85,000 \times 0.3 = 57,000$
Option 4 $\quad 40,000 \times 0.2 + 70,000 \times 0.5 + 125,000 \times 0.3 = 80,500$

Option 3 would thus be chosen as it gives the best expected cost using the best estimate of likely possibilities. Naturally, this estimate may be revised as fresh information is obtained, and the technique known as Bayes Theorem provides a way of doing this.

Proper handling of risks depends upon the most accurate measurement possible of severity and probability. Both depend upon efficient identification and the availability of the maximum amount of useful data from the past recorded in a systematic form which can be used conveniently to help predict the future.

6. Risk handling decisions

Once the activities of a business have been analysed and the risks which it faces have been identified and measured systematically, it is possible to begin to consider how these risks may best be handled.

Classification of risks

Measurement will have produced two values, one for the probability or frequency of the risk, the other for its severity. As we have already seen, a link will usually be found between these two measurements, a high frequency normally being found with low severity, low frequency with medium severity, and very low frequency with high severity.

In deciding the appropriate treatment for a risk the severity measurement is the more useful, and the correlation that exists between the two types of measurement permits assumptions to be made about relative severity where only the frequency can be measured – as might be the case where a record has been kept of the number of incidents, but the cost of those incidents has not been recorded separately.

Risks of low severity present few problems of management, especially when they are combined with a high frequency. The level of predictability is good, and these factors make it possible to identify readily what can be done to reduce the risk, or to limit its severity even more, and to budget to meet these costs in the same way as other recurrent expenses of the business.

The main risk handling problem lies in deciding what can be done about the risks of high severity and low frequency. These are the most unpredictable risks, but they are also the risks which embody the greatest threat to the continued existence of the business. The decision to allocate risks into their various severity classes is thus the first risk handling decision that must be made.

Methods of handling risk

The next decision is to determine, by reference to the general indications given by the severity classification and the particular features of the risk, as revealed by the identification and measurement charting procedure, which of the various risk handling devices is most likely to be appropriate for the particular risk.

There are four broad strategies to choose from: avoidance, control, transfer and financing.

Avoidance

Avoidance is the first strategy to be considered. It may be possible sometimes to eliminate the risk altogether by abandoning an operation or project, or contracting it out to a specialist. Alternatively, there may be ways of carrying out the operation differently, or in another place or using different plant or materials which will avoid the risk.

This method of risk handling has its limitations. In the first place, while a specific risk may be avoided, the changes necessary for that to occur will necessarily alter the risk pattern of the enterprise, and avoiding one risk may introduce new ones, while altering the probability and potential severity of others.

Secondly, while the option of avoidance is often available in managing speculative risk, it is less frequently a practicable option with pure risks. It is not easy to stop manufacturing a profitable product, or to relocate an established factory on pure risk grounds. The risk manager usually has to accept that risk avoidance is not a course open to him unless the change involved can be achieved without great cost or inconvenience. This will normally limit avoidance to specific parts of a process or to changes in the use of particular materials.

Control

Control is the risk manager's main method of combating risk. The basic question, "What happens if . . .?" implies, as we have seen, further questions about the severity and probability of risk, but finding answers to these questions serves little purpose unless a further question is asked: "What can we do about it?" If avoidance is not possible, then the risk manager must see what can be done at an economic cost to reduce the risk.

This can be done in one of two ways. Either the probability of the loss occurring can be reduced or action can be taken to limit its severity if it should occur. Because of the correlation between probability and severity, it may be possible by using either method, or a combination of them, to bring the potential loss down into a lower category of severity.

The means to be used may be either organisational or physical. In the former case, rearranging the way in which certain tasks are carried out, or making certain people responsible for seeing that particular precautions are taken, may reduce the risk. The latter case involves the installation of equipment to reduce loss. Fire detection and extinguishing appliances, or machine guards and interlocks are examples. In re-evaluating the risk with such protections, however, it is important not to fall into the error of assuming that because the devices have been installed, they will necessarily always be operating. Over-dependence on the operation of protective devices may, in some cases, warrant inclusion as an aggravating factor in the risk identification chart.

Transfer

Transfer of the risk itself by, for example, arranging for a hazardous process to be carried out by someone else, is a form of risk avoidance. There is, however, another form of transfer available to the risk manager – to transfer not the risk itself, but its financial effects. This can sometimes be achieved through contractual conditions which require the other party to give indemnity against certain types of liability or loss or damage, but it is important, if this course is adopted, to make certain that the other party will be in a position to meet his obligations if called upon to do so. Unless this is done, the risk may in fact only have been transferred on paper and may return to threaten the organisation which, because it had put too much faith in the effectiveness of the transfer, may be unprepared to meet it. The most common form of contractual transfer of this kind is, however, by insurance, whereby the insurer agrees to assume specified risks in return for a premium.

Financing

Financing cannot truly be considered an alternative to the three strategies mentioned above, since it includes insurance, which is a special form of risk transfer. In a soundly planned risk management programme it will reinforce the other measures selected. However good the system of loss control may be, it is very unlikely that a risk can be eliminated by it. Transfer, whether by insurance or other means, is also unlikely to be so effective that the consequences of the risk could not involve the organisation in some form of direct or indirect loss, interruption or inconvenience. In virtually every case, therefore, there will be residual or contingent risks for which a financing plan is necessary. Insurance is an important risk financing tool, but it is not the complete answer to risks, and is all too often used to finance the wrong category of risks. A full financing programme will, therefore, be made up of a combination of providing for risks in normal operating budgets, self-insurance plans, insurance and possibly other less common financing methods, such as contingent lines of credit.

Dealing with specific risks

Once the most appropriate methods of treatment for a particular risk have been determined, the third of the main risk handling decisions has to be made. That will be to decide the details of a plan to deal with each specific risk.

In order to make this decision, reference must be made back to the components of the risk identification chart. One must look at the consequences of the occurrence of the risk in detail and predict both the direct and the indirect consequences. Next, the cost of those direct and indirect consequences must be calculated and examined closely to see whether it would vary significantly if the loss were to happen at a particular time, or in particular circumstances. If there is such a variation, the worst possible situation must be catered for in the risk treatment programme, for pessimism in matters of risk is the only prudent philosophy.

The potential cost is only one of the factors which will determine the appropriate plan for treating the risk. It will also be necessary to establish both the probability of loss and the predictability of its occurrence. The risks which threaten an organisation are rarely of a kind for which it is possible to calculate exact probabilities. With the smaller losses, which happen more frequently and for which there is likely to be a larger body of data, the law of large numbers can be of considerable help. Briefly, this law can be expressed as stating that the greater the number of events of the same kind that are observed, the closer will the results approximate to the true probability. Given a sufficient data base, some assumptions can be made about the underlying probability, which will be extremely useful in deciding how the risk should be handled. In theory, of course, the events considered should all be of the same type, but for practical purposes it is not always necessary that they be exactly homogeneous. No useful information about the probability of fire, for example, can be deduced from the record of a group of 500 buildings, identical in every respect, in which there has never been a fire. Data about 500 fire losses in non-identical buildings may, however, enable some rough assessment of the probability to be made.

When it comes to major risks which would endanger the continued existence of the organisation, theoretical probabilities are of little value. Comparable events occur relatively rarely, so that there is an insufficient base to allow any calculations to be made, and since a catastrophe of this kind, if unprovided for, might well mean the end of the organisation it can, from the organisation's point of view, be treated as a unique event. In such a case, attempting to determine the exact probability is both impossible and unnecessary. All that needs to be noted is that if the probability is greater than zero then a decision will have to be taken as to how the risk should best be handled. It is easy – perhaps fatally easy – to assume a major risk away and to imagine that because the probability, although unknown, must be extremely low, it can therefore be treated as being zero.

Personal factors

Risk handling decisions are likely to be affected by the outlook of the person called upon to make them, for different people have different views on the attitude to adopt when faced with risk.

There are two aspects to this psychological modification of what would otherwise be a straightforward assessment of the probabilities, followed by a decision flowing logically from that assessment. There is, first of all, subjective probability. In making a decision relating to a possible future occurrence, the true statistical probability may be an important factor, but each person will have his own set of preconceptions about the weight that is to be given to the probability figures and it is on the basis of this subjectively higher or lower probability that the decision will be taken. Most people, for example, underestimate the dangers of travel by car and overestimate those of travel by aircraft. One might term this subjective probability a "nevertheless factor", since it commonly expresses itself in thoughts such as "I know it's ten thousand to one against it happening, but nevertheless I won't take any chances", or, "There is a chance things may go wrong, nevertheless I will take the risk."

The estimation of subjective probabilities is very much a matter of temperament. The other psychological factor in decision taking, however, while it is normally also instinctive, could conceivably be modified to conform with a set policy laid down by the organisation for the way in which decisions should be made. Every person has more or less of the gambler in them, which will determine whether they are prepared to take risks or will be predisposed to look for safety. This attitude will not be constant even in one person, for it may vary at different times of life, with different kinds of possibilities and with the amount at stake – most people who would willingly risk a small amount on a very remote chance would require a much greater probability of success if the loss would mean total ruin. In the same way, someone might identify the security of their job with the avoidance of unexpected losses and be less prepared to take risk on behalf of the organisation than they might have done on their own account; conversely, they might be far more ready to risk the organisation's money than their own.

It is possible to detect a trend in modern business towards a more cautious approach to risk, which runs parallel with the decline in importance of the individual entrepreneur – who was temperamentally inclined to take a chance, and was, to a large extent, his company – and the rise of the large corporation, administered by professional managers and accountants. One can draw an analogy with the world of sport. There was a time when Ian Hay could write:"The tortoise is a terribly unpopular winner . . . a real hero is a man who wins a championship in the morning, despite the fact that he was dead drunk the night before."* In other words, the risk taker was an admired character, in sport as in business. Since then, however, there has been a change in attitude among players, associated with the growing rewards to be found in sport, so that "professionalism" has ceased to be a pejorative term and has become one of admiration. In the big-money sports, such as tennis and golf, the successful players have increasingly been those who "play the percentages": that is to say, those who reduce risk by shots which can be relied on

---

The Lighter Side of School Life, Hodder & Stoughton, 1922.

to give satisfactory results most of the time, or which minimise the chances of an opponent being able to make an unexpected reply. Sport has become big business and the readiness to accept risk has been reduced as more is at stake.

It must also be recognised that, whereas in theory a decision maker might be expected always to seek to make the decision which gives the optimum result, he may in fact set his sights much lower and seek some lesser return which he considers satisfactory. Another sporting example will illustrate this. A professional football team, particularly playing away, may very often aim not at the optimum result of a win, but at the satisfactory result of a draw, and will therefore base its strategy on the efficient avoidance of defeat. It will win if the opportunity presents itself, but its aspirations will be satisfied if it achieves the draw.

Risk handling decisions, like any others, will be affected by these factors and by the interaction of the personalities of those in command which together make up the corporate attitude to risk and management style. At the same time, it is worth remembering that the company's organisational manuals – if its management style lends itself to such things – are unlikely to spell out the corporate attitude to risk, and that individual decisions may be affected by the personal degree of risk aversion of the particular decision maker. This may be very different from that of the company as a whole.

The risk manager therefore needs to be aware of the approach to risk of individual members of senior management, as well as the consensus of their views which forms the corporate attitude to risk. Both will be important in determining the degree of caution that needs to be built into a risk management programme if it is to fit the organisation's character. If it fails to do that, then no matter how logical the risk handling decision may be in theory, or how accurate the statistical base on which it was taken, it will not be the right one for the company.

The nature of the organisation itself will influence its overall attitude to risk. A non profit-making organisation whose main objective is the uninterrupted supply of a service will be less inclined to take risks than an entrepreneurial company whose main aim is short-term profit to satisfy the expectations of shareholders. A company which is highly decentralised, whether because it is a multinational or because it has a broad product range, may find it difficult to utilise its full capacity for risk retention. This is because its pure risk decisions tend to be made locally in the context of the individual division or subsidiary.

A family business which puts a high value on continuity may be more cautious about risk than a publicly owned company whose horizons are bounded to a much greater extent by the annual results it must present to its shareholders. A large company can be expected to have more risk management options open to it than a small company in a comparable state of financial health, although risk management can, of course, help both. The large company will probably have a better spread of risk and greater financial resources, which will give it more scope to retain risk, and it is likely to be able to employ specialists in various aspects of risk control, while the smaller company will be more dependent upon insurance and on the services of outside consultants.

The right risk handling decision will thus depend on many factors which will be different for each company. Apart from the generalisation that catastrophic risks must be transferred if economically possible, one cannot therefore lay down firm rules for choosing between risk handling options. All one can say is that the decision must fit the individual company's nature, aims and risk attitude. If it fails to do that, then it has a poor chance of success, however correct it may seem in theory.

7. Financing potential loss

Risk transfer

In the previous chapter we traced the series of decisions which must be taken as part of the process of risk management. We have seen that after risks have been sorted into their various categories of severity, there are a number of alternative methods of dealing with risk from which to choose. In broad terms, however, the choice resolves itself into a selection of one of two strategies: either to accept a possible loss, or to arrange some form of financing procedure to meet the loss when it occurs.

As we have seen, potential severity is the factor which should govern the decision whether a risk is to be accepted or financed. Risk acceptance should be reserved for risks of low severity and risks should never be accepted inadvertently or without due consideration of their possible effects on the organisation. Risk management exists to provide a technique for ensuring that risks are discovered and evaluated systematically, so that the appropriate handling method may be chosen.

Non-insurance transfer

Let us first look at transfer of risk other than by insurance. The aim here is to finance the cost of potential loss by ensuring that if a loss occurs someone else will have the responsibility of paying for it. The usual method of attempting to achieve this is by means of exclusion or indemnity clauses in contracts, but this is far from being a certain way of freeing oneself from the financial consequences of a risk. Such conditions can, of course, only be enforced against a party to the contract, and only then if it can be proved that the clause formed part of the contract when it was made.

The courts have shown their dislike of exclusion clauses by putting the narrowest possible interpretation on them, and legislation has restricted their use still further. The Unfair Contract Terms Act 1977 renders void contractual terms which restrict or exclude liability for death or personal injury resulting from negligence, and only permits restrictions on liability for other loss or damage by negligence if the clause can be considered reasonable. In deciding whether such a clause is reasonable or not, the circumstances in which the contract was entered into, the relative bargaining power of each party, whether such clauses were normal in the trade and any other relevant facts will be taken into account.

Where goods are sold to the public, the act prohibits attempts to contract out of the implied warranties of merchantable quality and fitness for purpose under the Sale of Goods Act 1979. In non-consumer sales, such clauses are permissible, but only if they are reasonable.

There are thus serious obstacles in the path of anyone seeking to use this form of risk transfer. Even if they can be surmounted, such a transfer is worth no more than the financial resources of the person to whom the risk is transferred. These may be adequate at the time the agreement is entered into, but in the absence of a continuous system of check, which may well be impracticable, one can never be certain that the risk has been effectively transferred.

Transfer by insurance

The mechanism of insurance will be considered in detail later in this book, but it must be included here as the most widely used method of financing risk. The introduction of systematic risk management into an organisation will often show that the purchase of insurance has in the past been poorly planned, if it has been planned at all. Risk management can often eliminate many insurances against events which would have only a minor effect upon the organisation, either financially or by interrupting the services which it is designed to provide.

The termination of these unnecessary insurances is often the first visible effect of risk management and this has led to the myth that risk management is anti-insurance. Nothing could be further from the truth. One of the most important constituents of risk management is the proper use of insurance, which means using it where it will be most effective as a financing technique, i.e. in areas of medium and large risk. To refuse to buy unnecessary insurance is not to be anti-insurance, but anti-waste of resources. The application of risk management principles indeed may not lead to an overall reduction in the amount of money spent on insurance premiums, for the funds that are released by cancelling unnecessary small covers may be used for catastrophe insurance in areas which have previously been overlooked or where cover was previously inadequate. By doing this, the organisation will be getting better value from its expenditure on insurance, since the expenditure will be concentrated where it can do the organisation most good.

Internal funding and the use of credit

If it is decided that the loss is neither to be financed by insurance nor to be accepted and paid for out of revenue, the financing possibilities are limited to a choice between internal funding and the use of credit, both of which have substantial disadvantages.

If a budget or fund is to be set up from which losses of a particular kind will be met, many of the insurers' costs and expenses, which would have to be paid for as part of a premium, can be avoided. At the same time, however, non-insurance organisations do not normally enjoy the advantages of insurers in making pre-tax reserves from which to pay for future losses. This imposes a penalty upon companies wishing to establish a fund which is carried forward from year to year. Such a fund can, however, have its uses. It provides a way of overcoming the problem of losses which are too large for individual profit centres to bear, but which are well within the capability of the organisation as a whole to retain. Such losses can be paid from a fund to which all sections of the organisation contribute as if they were paying an outside insurance premium. The advantage of maintaining an internal fund is that contributions can be varied, not only in accordance with the record of each contributor, but also with the changing financial state of the company, with additional central transfers being made to it in good times so that contributions perhaps may be suspended in bad times.

There can be administrative problems, however, with such a fund. Criteria for the acceptance of claims against the fund must be laid down, and internal standards of proof of loss should not be less stringent than those an insurer would apply. Unless this is done, the fund may be exploited by the wilier parts of the organisation as a useful additional budget or contingency fund.

There is also the danger that if there is a healthy balance in the fund for several years, and claims upon it are low, it may be "borrowed" to finance other activities within the organisation, so that when the more serious claims come along, the fund is insufficient to meet them.

The fund, too, must be adequately financed when it is set up. If it has to rely on the gradual accumulation of funds from contributions, the organisation may find itself insufficiently protected against an unexpected run of claims early in the fund's life.

The alternative method of non-insurance financing of risk is to borrow the funds necessary to meet losses as they arise. This is a method which is not often chosen, because the fluctuations of the credit market may mean a lower degree of certainty that funds will be available to meet a loss than may be required. This is particularly true if recourse is made to normal credit facilities to meet a loss. Not only may the loss occur at a time when the amount of credit available is restricted, but the loss itself, if it happens to be of a major asset, may diminish the organisation's bargaining power in seeking further credit.

An alternative possibility is to arrange a contingent line of credit in advance, to be drawn on in the event of a loss. This may be difficult to arrange on terms which are acceptable, and either form of credit, while it protects cash flow and earnings by spreading the loss over the period of borrowing, still results in a depletion of net assets.

Evaluating financing methods

In comparing the cost of other financing methods with that of insurance, it is important to remember that there are secondary costs involved, whichever method is selected, which may not be exactly quantifiable in advance, but which must be considered if any comparison of methods is to be meaningful. If insurance is selected it is important to anticipate the reaction of the insurance market to a large loss. Would the insurers, in these circumstances, be likely to terminate the insurance, or to require severely increased premiums for the future? It will be very much better for an organisation to consider such possibilities at the outset, rather than to wait until the loss has happened and then be forced to consider the problem at a time when its freedom of manoeuvre will be much more restricted.

The effect that damage to, or loss of, a key asset might have upon the stock market must also be carefully considered if the organisation is a quoted company. The share price in relation to other comparable companies tends to be the barometer by which the management of a company is judged, and the market wants to see a continued and uninterrupted flow of earnings. Loss of an important asset, even if it is insured, may be taken to imply a loss of earning power during the period until it is reinstated, and this reaction may be even sharper if the company has decided to finance the loss other than through insurance. In both cases, therefore, and particularly in the second, adequate contingency planning for continued operation without the asset is essential. It is also essential to be able to demonstrate that this planning has taken place and is reliable if market confidence is to be preserved.

In much the same way, reduction in the earning capacity of a company may adversely affect its borrowing facilities at a time when its resources are already strained. This is a strong argument against relying on normal sources of finance for credit from which to meet a loss. Evidence of constructive contingency planning to minimise the effects of the loss may be invaluable in retaining the confidence of the credit market.

In selecting an appropriate financing strategy, attention must also be paid to the possible timing of the loss. The differing effects upon a seasonal business of a loss at different times of the year can easily be appreciated, and it would be unwise to do other than to base one's calculations on the assumption that the loss will occur at the worst possible time of the year. There are, however, other factors that can make the timing of a loss important, which apply to any sort of organisation. The effects of a loss may be magnified if it occurs at the peak or at the lowest point of a trading cycle, whether of the organisation itself or of the economy as a whole. The possibility of the loss coinciding with restrictions upon credit have been touched on above, and the effects of a loss could also vary according to fluctuation in the supply of labour or materials for rebuilding, or of replacement parts or machinery.

Each of these factors, and many others particular to the organisation, will be relevant in deciding the appropriate financing method, and they impose upon an organisation the necessity of trying to resolve two uncertainties: the probability of the loss occurring, and of its occurrence coinciding with the worst possible internal or external situation.

The convention of the accounting year is also a limiting factor in selecting methods of financing loss. The concept of an accounting year is very useful for comparative purposes, and for measuring the progress of an organisation. At the same time, however, most organisations have either a continuous life, or the expectation of a continuous life. The stronger this expectation, the less relevant results over a period as short as one year can become. If, on the other hand, there is doubt about the future of the business, a period of a year may be far too long to be meaningful.

The embarrassment which a medium-sized loss may cause a company largely arises because its effects have to be shown against the results in a single year. If there were no necessity to account for the company's results every twelve months, it would be easier to recognise losses of medium size for what they really are. In the context of the whole life of the company, they are insignificant, and capable of being borne without jeopardising the continued existence of the organisation. The importance of geographical spread of risk is reasonably well understood as a factor in deciding how potential losses are best financed. The principle of chronological spread, however, is equally valid, and if a device can be found to spread a loss over several years of an organisation's existence it may be possible to treat it as being of a lesser relative severity.

The full range of financial techniques is only slowly being applied to the area traditionally thought of as the province of insurance. As more sophisticated techniques are used, so the range of alternative methods of financing loss will be extended. Insurance, however, seems likely to remain the most important single financing method and we shall be examining its techniques in some detail in the next chapter.

8. The insurance mechanism

One of the chief problems that risk management has had to overcome has been to differentiate itself from insurance, partly because of the insurance background of many of the pioneers in risk management thinking, and partly because risk – at least those varieties of it with which risk management is chiefly concerned – has for so long been considered the preserve of insurance alone. The confusion has been perpetuated because insurance retains such an important role as the main method of risk financing in a risk management programme.

Risk management does not supersede insurance, but puts it in its proper perspective, as fulfilling a useful function determined after critical assessment of what it has to offer compared with other financing possibilities. To get the best out of any risk management programme, therefore, requires a knowledge of how the insurance mechanism works, and an appreciation of ways in which the insurance industry treats the risk passed on to it in return for the premium paid.

For the purchaser, insurance provides a method of smoothing loss experience over a period of time, by exchanging the pure risk which is insured for the smaller risk of the failure of the insurer to settle a claim when it is made, either through lack of funds or by some breach of the conditions of the insurance contract by the insured himself.

Except for the small insured, or the catastrophic loss, it is unlikely that the cost of loss will be permanently transferred from the insured to the insurer; for the latter will seek to recover what he has paid out by increased premiums in subsequent years. Indeed, he may already have recovered it in previous years when the premiums paid have been greater than the amount needed to pay claims and meet the insurer's expenses.

Where there is sufficient supply of insurance and where insurers are competing strongly for business, it may be possible to defer or avoid repayment of the cost of loss by changing insurers, but in most cases this will be only a short-term solution, unless there has been some substantial improvement in loss control to improve the probable future cost of loss. A new insurer may offer a lower premium, taking the chance that the loss experience will improve, but if it does not, then the premium cost is likely to rise to, and perhaps beyond, its old level.

The service of chronological loss spreading is, however, what the insured really needs, even if the total cost is not thereby reduced, for it enables him to reduce the annual cost of large losses to a size at which they can be borne in a single accounting year.

From the insurer's point of view, the risk that is transferred to him has a different aspect. What was a pure risk for the insured becomes a speculative risk for the insurer, for in his hands it presents possibilities either of profit or of loss. The fact that a reinsurance market exists as a method of treating this risk is, however, a reminder that pure risk and insurable risk are not synonymous terms.

Risk spreading

The methods the insurer uses to treat the risk he carries are themselves a good example of risk management in action. He seeks first of all to diminish his risk by ensuring that it is well spread. This is achieved in a number of ways. First, a good spread of risk is sought by endeavouring to ensure that the portfolio he is insuring consists of a large number of similar items. This will give the greatest play to the operation of the law of large numbers, and thus improve the predictability of the loss experience. Next, the insurers will wish these insurances to come from many different locations to provide the necessary geographical spread to minimise the chance of an abnormal loss experience due to a localised catastrophe.

This is the classic picture of the insurer as the collector of contributions from many to pay for the losses of the few that suffer them. It is still a true picture for many smaller types of insurances, but the changing nature of risk is reducing its validity, as we shall see, for many of the more potentially catastrophic types of risk.

As well as spreading risk geographically in this way, the insurer also seeks to spread it chronologically, by building up reserves for future losses – a process which is easier in nearly all countries for an insurer than for any other type of company which might like to do the same from its own funds. An insurer, unlike other companies, is permitted to set up reserves of this kind out of pre-tax earnings. This fact has been one of the attractions of setting up a captive insurance company as part of a risk financing programme.

Risk financing and transfer

In financing his risks, the insurer adopts sound risk management tactics in retaining only that part of the potential loss which can comfortably be borne in a single accounting year. The existence of the reinsurance market, which is designed to provide exactly this service to the direct insurer, makes it simple for him to buy cover for the larger and catastrophic risk only.

Rating systems

In deciding on the premium to charge, insurers make use of three main rating systems. The first of these, *class rating,* is applicable to those risks where the insurer has in his portfolio a large number of broadly similar cases. In practice, they will rarely be identical, and the hazard each presents, and thus the premium which should equitably be paid for it, will vary. The insurer, therefore, subdivides the range of cases into a number of groups and decides on the appropriate premium to be paid by an average case within each group. Greater and lesser hazard in individual cases within the group is then recognised by increased or decreased premiums in relation to the average.

Class rating is easy to apply and provides rough justice between one insured and another, as well as a means, for small insurance customers, of spreading loss amongst them, but it has the disadvantage that it offers comparatively little recognition to the insured who is substantially better than the average, so that the insured whose loss control is excellent may well find himself subsidising the poor risks in the same class, even if the premium paid is the minimum for the class.

Where the number of comparable insurances is small, or where one cover is so large by comparison with others in its class that its results would affect those of the class unduly, *experience rating* is used. This system, under which the premium depends upon the past experience of the individual insured, provides the insured essentially with a chronological loss spreading service for his losses, since the insured will be expected, over time, to repay at least the non-catastrophic losses which the insurer has paid, together with the insurer's expenses of handling them.

This system gives more credit to the good, or lucky, insured, and penalises the insured with a poor record more surely than class rating. With changes in technology, more and more industrial processes are becoming concentrated into a much smaller number of units. Advantage may be derived from the economies of scale while all goes well, but the potential loss in the event of a serious stoppage will probably be increased by the reduction in the number of alternative sources of supply. This reduction will also make class rating less suitable, because the number of members of each class will shrink, and as they become larger, they are likely to develop distinctive features which will make the classification less appropriate.

In many cases, however, the risk is not only concentrated, but also not strictly comparable with anything in the past – it may, for example be on a larger scale, or the technology may be entirely new, or it may raise new questions about the boundaries of legal liability. In such a case, experience rating will not serve either and the insurer has to rely on some form of *subjective rating*. This term can cover anything from a rate based on detailed analysis of the probabilities involved to one based on pure guesswork. Objectively, the rates fixed in this way may prove to be too high or too low – subsequent experience showed that the premiums initially fixed for wide-bodied jet aircraft, for example, were too high; those for supertankers or satellites too low. Subjective ratings can create an insurance market for a new risk, or if they are too high when measured against the risk as assessed by the potential insured, they are increasingly likely to encourage him to seek some alternative method of financing the risk, probably by entering the specialist insurance market himself or in conjunction with others in the same industry.

Mutuals and captives

Dissatisfaction with insurers' rating methods is a common reason for the establishment of mutual or captive insurance companies. In fact many companies which have started out in this way have developed into important parts of the conventional insurance market, although they owe their foundation to dissatisfaction with that market. Others have found the inflexibility of the insurance market, notably in refusing to offer cover of the extent, or on conditions, that the client requires, to be a good reason for going into the insurance business themselves, and in this way to widen the variety of wares that are available in the market.

Direct access to the reinsurance market has also been an incentive for the formation of captive insurance companies. It is a wholesale market, and therefore cheaper; it is much more closely experience-rated, and therefore fairer to the large risk; and it provides cover particularly for the large and catastrophic risk, which is the protection that risk management, as we have seen, looks for from insurance. Direct insurers, although buying their own insurance protection in exactly this way, have in the past been reluctant to sell this kind of protection to their clients – they have preferred to sell cover from the ground up rather than offer large deductibles, and excess of loss and stop-loss covers have not been made readily available.

There has been a change in attitude in recent years, which has been encouraged by the buyer's market which developed in insurance. Faced with intense competition from conventional insurers and the proliferation of captives, the market found that it could, after all, offer deductibles and the retrospective rating plans and similar chronological loss-spreading devices that risk managers were demanding. The change of heart was first seen among American insurers but, under the pressure of competition, the British market followed suit. Whether, as a seller's market re-establishes itself, insurers will seek to revert to their older ways, remains to be seen.

The insurance mechanism is vital to risk management, where its function is to finance large risks. This requires forms of insurance tailored to this particular need, which, as we have seen, can be created. Insurance thinking, however, is still conditioned to a large extent by a conception of its role as the spreading of relatively small risks. For the individual, insurance is often indispensable; for the large industrial concern, it is but one risk management tool among many, to be used where its contribution is most valuable as a means of transferring the financial effects of large and catastrophic risks.

9. Captive insurance companies

In the discussion on insurance in the last chapter, some reference was made to the popularity of "do it yourself" insurance in the form of captive insurance companies. Although the creation of many such companies has been one of the most important features of insurance over the past 20 years, there is nothing particularly new in the idea. The history of insurance is studded with companies which began as subsidiaries of firms not primarily engaged in insurance, or as mutual associations of a number of such firms. Some of those formed in this way have developed into large and respected members of the conventional insurance market.

Generally speaking, they were formed either because it was felt that rates for a particular company or industry were too high, or because some cover considered to be essential was either not available from the insurance market in the form in which it was wanted, or was only available on terms that were thought unreasonable.

Reasons for captives

It is an apparent anomaly of insurance that very large groups should look for protection to insurance companies which may be many times smaller than themselves. There are three main reasons why they should do so. First, the purchase of insurance is a convenient way of spreading the cost of major losses over several years. A company could achieve this objective by setting up a reserve fund to meet potential losses, but in all but a very few countries it would not be able to do so out of pre-tax earnings. This tax disincentive does not apply to insurers, and since insurance premiums are tax-deductible while contributions to an internal fund are not, this is a second reason for insuring.

The third reason which makes insurance possible despite disparity in size between insured and insurer is the existence of the international reinsurance market, which permits even a small insurer to accept large risks and to spread them among other insurers. They in turn may reinsure further, so that insurers in every continent may eventually share the cost of a major disaster. Each of these three reasons has, as we shall see, some bearing on the popularity of captives.

It must first be conceded, however, that there was an element of following fashion in the establishment of many of the captives formed in the 1970s. For some companies, the captive was a rather glamorous corporate extension, and not to have one was to be missing something, regardless of whether it could strictly be justified objectively from a risk management point of view.

Growth in the number of captives was undoubtedly also stimulated by heavy promotion by companies specialising in managing them. Nevertheless, the major factor in the growth of captives – a growth so great that Bermuda alone now houses a captive for every 57 inhabitants – has been the realisation that to form a captive is a logical extension of self-insurance as part of a risk management approach to countering the threats which face a company.

What large companies need most from insurance is relief from the financial burden of a catastrophic loss, and a means of spreading losses which, although smaller, would still be too great to be brought conveniently into a single year's accounts, over a longer period. Self-funding would be attractive, were it not for the tax penalty, but, at the time of the boom in captives, the tax authorities made no distinction between an insurance company owned by its policyholders, even if it underwrote no other risks, and one which was entirely independent. As premiums were tax-deductible, whether paid to a conventional insurance company or to a subsidiary, logic as well as inclination pointed in many cases to the formation of a captive insurance company.

Such a company could not retain more than a very small proportion of its parent's risks without being very heavily capitalised, were it not for the existence of the reinsurance market to which its status as an insurer gives it access. This access is one of the main advantages of captive insurance. The reinsurance market is a wholesale one and therefore cheaper, since it does not have to carry the volume of overheads, in the form of such things as acquisition costs, branch networks and survey services, which direct insurers have to meet. Moreover, in the case of excess of loss reinsurance, which is what the captive will most commonly require, the reinsurer only becomes involved when the captive's own retention is exhausted, so that the rate charged for reinsurance does not have to reflect the cost of small claims.

Reinsurance is experience-rated; therefore the captive, and hence its parent, will be rated on its own performance, so that good risk management reflected in a low loss record will be better and much more quickly rewarded than would be the case in the direct insurance market. There is, of course, the corresponding disadvantage that any falling-off of standards will be much more quickly penalised. Reinsurance, too, is a market for professionals, and most captives will need specialised advice in placing their reinsurance programme.

Reinsurance captives

It has become increasingly common for captives to be set up as re-insurance companies rather than as direct insurers. The simple method of operation whereby the captive issues a policy to its parent, and then reinsures all risk in excess of that which it can safely retain, may sometimes be impossible. This is commonly the case where the parent company is a multinational. Many countries forbid the insurance of risks in their territory with insurers who are not licensed to do business there. It may be compulsory to insure with a state insurer, or local laws, language and insurance practice may present problems.

Problems of this kind can often be solved if the captive is part of the international reinsurance market. In such cases, the captive will arrange for a policy to be issued by an approved local insurer, which will reinsure some or all of the risk with the captive, which will itself reinsure the balance that it cannot retain with other reinsurers.

Operation

It has always been desirable that, whatever form it takes, a captive should be conceived and operated as a genuine insurance company. With tax authorities showing distinct hostility to captives operating in any other way, it is now essential.

In the USA, the Internal Revenue Service has won a number of decisions in the courts disallowing tax relief on premiums paid to "pure" captives which underwrite only their parent companies' risks. The reasoning is that insurance transactions involving only members of the same economic family lack the essential quality of risk transfer which characterises true insurance. As a result, American-owned captives have sought hurriedly, and in some cases disastrously, to diversify into accepting outside risks, thus becoming more like conventional insurance companies. Another effect has been to change the emphasis of captive formation to group or association captives, where a number of companies form a joint insurance company.

Captives have always been limited in the extent to which they can operate in a manner unlike that of conventional insurers because as soon as a captive requires any form of reinsurance, it will be dealing with that conventional market, and will be expected to conform to its accepted standards.

Preconditions for success

It therefore follows that, in order to be accepted and successful, a captive must fulfil certain preconditions. If its parents are to be certain that forming a captive will improve their risk financing programme, a thorough feasibility study will first be necessary. The first essential is that the captive is set up as part of a concerted approach to the problem of risk. This will imply that techniques of risk identification and evaluation must be well developed in the organisation, so that the captive may be used to finance the most appropriate risks.

A good and well-documented loss record will be necessary if the captive is to be able to offer acceptable business to the reinsurance market. This must be maintained by efficient loss control techniques within the parent company. If the loss record is poor, then the improvement of loss control is the first priority, not the formation of a captive, which will always want to be able to present its risks to the reinsurance market as being better than the average.

The volume of premium must be sufficient to make the captive worth while, and there must be an adequate spread of risk within the parent organisation. This may well mean that only some of the parent's risks can be placed with the captive, at least in its early years. Where there is a heavy concentration of risk at one location, it may be preferable to place that risk in the conventional insurance market, where the presence of other similar risks can provide the spread that the captive would lack.

It will also be necessary for there to be sufficiently unified control over the placing of insurance in the parent company for full use to be made of the captive for those risks for which it is best suited.

Finally, the captive must be properly managed, and very commonly a professional management company which specialises in operating captives is used, especially when the captive is to be located in one of the offshore centres for this type of insurance.

Types of captive

The "pure" captive has fewer complications than one which accepts outside risks, and for this reason it was the most common choice during the captive boom. It has the advantage of an excellent knowledge of the risks it underwrites, but its spread of risk is inevitably limited. The attitude of tax authorities is now, however, making this a less popular choice.

A captive writing open market business must be very selective in its underwriting or it may find itself a dumping-ground for the worst risks in the market, so a popular way of entering the captive market is by a joint venture with other companies in the same industry. This avoids the problems of the captive which derives all its premium from its parent, but only at the expense of introducing operational problems.

Rating can be a bone of contention between partners when their loss records are not uniformly good, and there may be greater difficulty in deciding which risks are most suitable for the captive to underwrite. The underwriting information which has to be passed to the captive may include confidential matters, and this can be a problem when the captive is owned jointly with a competitor. Suitable provisions must also be made for procedures to be followed if one partner or another wishes to opt out of the arrangement, because the sudden withdrawal of a substantial part of the risks insured could unbalance the captive's underwriting portfolio seriously.

Offshore locations

The history of the development of captive insurance in recent years has very much been the history of the offshore captives. Low rates of corporate tax, enabling a captive's funds to be built up much more quickly, and the ability to defer tax on profits until they are remitted to the parent company have played a large part in the choice of offshore locations, but they are not the whole story.

The difficulties involved in forming new insurance companies in most countries have also been a significant influence. Most of the legislative requirements are designed to protect policyholders and are therefore of limited relevance to those forming captives, who find formalities in the offshore captive centres more attractive for being simpler. As the importance of captives in world insurance has grown, however, the need for some basic legislation to ensure adequate capitalisation of captives and their operation as bona fide insurance companies has been appreciated by those territories seeking to establish themselves, through captives, as important insurance centres.

Bermuda is overwhelmingly the most important centre for captive insurance companies. It was there that the major US-led expansion of captives took place, and the island has now become a recognised international insurance centre. Captives, however, are to be found in many other low tax areas. Guernsey established itself as a popular choice for British companies during the period when exchange control regulations ruled out Bermuda for them and made it necessary to find a location within the Sterling Area in which to form captives. There is now once again a free choice, and many other territories have been suggested as possible locations, but Bermuda, the Cayman Islands and Guernsey still house the vast majority of offshore captives.

These centres can provide all the management, accounting and legal services which are necessary for captives, and adequate communications with other world markets for them to be credible bases for an insurance company. The same cannot yet be said for some of the more exotic locations which have been suggested.

Disadvantages of captives

The popularity of captives may be such as to mislead a company into thinking that no risk management programme can be complete without one. It is wise to look at the disadvantages as well as the advantages before deciding whether a captive is appropriate in a particular case.

First, the outlook for captives is by no means unclouded. The American tax authorities' attack on pure captives has been followed in the UK by the controlled foreign company legislation introduced in the Finance Act 1984. This permits the Inland Revenue to charge UK corporation tax on the profits of an offshore captive unless certain conditions are fulfilled, of which the only two of general application are that either the captive must remit at least 50 per cent of its profits annually to the UK, or it must derive at least 50 per cent of its income from underwriting risks unconnected with its parent. This legislation does not make captive insurance impossible, but the introduction of restrictions of this kind must raise the question of whether they may be made more stringent in the future.

Secondly, a captive will, in any event, involve tying up a certain amount of capital, because adequate capitalisation is essential for a captive as for any other insurance company. It may also make heavy demands upon management time, particularly in its early days, and its existence may possibly offend actual or potential investors in the parent. The necessity to provide adequate services for the captive may prove troublesome and, as has been mentioned above, the volatility and rating methods of the reinsurance market may mean that the effect of a sudden deterioration in the parent's loss pattern could be more marked and more immediate.

Finally, although dissatisfaction with the existing insurance market may be a reason for the formation of many captives, there are limits to the extent to which a captive can be unorthodox. The risks it undertakes must be at least potentially insurable in the conventional market, unless the captive proposes to retain them in full, because the reinsurance market's criteria of acceptability will be broadly the same as those of direct insurers. Similarly, the captive's rates must bear at least some relation to those current in the market, not only for the credibility of the captive in the insurance world, but also to forestall any objections from the tax authorities that payments made by the captive are not genuine insurance premiums.

Conclusion

Properly constituted and used, captive insurance companies provide an excellent financing tool for use in a co-ordinated risk management programme. They must not be treated lightly as gimmicks or as purely tax-avoidance devices. To operate a captive is to become part of the world-wide insurance industry, and it is a step to be taken only after proper consideration. Above all, a captive is not a substitute for proper loss control; on the contrary, it reinforces the need for it.

10. Loss control

Good loss control lies at the centre of any effective risk management programme. Without an efficient system to ensure that losses are kept to the minimum that is achievable by measures which are economically feasible, there is likely to be too much fluctuation in loss records from one year to another for risk financing decisions to be taken on the basis of data that are sufficiently reliable.

The dangers of specialisation

All organisations are likely to practise some form of loss control, but all too often the effort is fragmented, and responsibilities for different aspects of it given to widely separated functions within the organisation, with no communication between them or overall co-ordination of their activities. Fire prevention, safety and security are the three aspects of loss control that receive most attention, and all too often they are the province of specialists, whose interest is bounded by the confines of their own specialisations. Such a narrow view, of course, reduces the efficiency of an effective overall loss control programme, which should involve every member of an organisation.

The aims of security and assured means of escape from fire, for example, frequently come into conflict, which may make it difficult for those engaged in the argument to appreciate that they are both essentially seeking different aspects of the same thing – a reduction in the possible loss of the organisation's assets, whether those assets be represented by property or by people.

Specialisation, too, makes it harder to recognise other allies in the same fight. The safety officer, for example, might well find it surprising to think of the work of a product designer or quality controller as being part of a similar loss control effort to his own, and all of them might be unaware of the loss control work of the organisation's legal department in checking the terms of contracts it enters into.

If properly applied, loss control is part of every activity in the organisation, reducing the probability of loss and increasing the probability of survival if the unexpected should occur.

Loss control and risk management

Since it should permeate the organisation and should be recognised as part of every job description, it is unfortunate that rigid specialisation has made it possible for one part of the loss control process to act in isolation from another. It is doubly unfortunate that loss control is also so often seen to be something entirely separate from other aspects of risk management. Indeed, there are many who say that loss control is risk management, and they are as misguided as those who claim that risk management means risk financing only. Risk management is no more safety management alone, or fire prevention alone, or security alone than it is self-insurance alone.

The problems of co-ordinating loss control within an organisation are very similar to those of co-ordinating risk management as a whole. If it is not seen as everyone's task, if it is left to the specialist to worry about, then he alone will have to carry the immense burden of trying to bring about, in the face of indifference or opposition from all around him, something that can only be achieved through co-operation.

The physical aspect

Good loss control has two aspects – the physical and the psychological. On the physical side are all the devices, whether tangible or organisational, which prevent the actual occurrence of an event giving rise to a loss, whether it concerns material damage, safety and health of employees and others, the security of premises, documents, data and information, potential liabilities arising from premises, products or the acts or omission of staff, or any other aspect of the business. The loss control devices available, particularly in the fields of fire and explosion detection, control and suppression, and of security systems, become increasingly complicated, and inevitably are more and more the work of experts in a narrow field. While their expertise should be respected, it is perhaps worth remembering that to rely wholly upon an expert of any kind is to open a gap in a loss control programme.

However effective the device that is installed, it is never a complete answer on its own to a loss control problem. Does it require periodic maintenance or inspection, and if so, is the property it normally protects vulnerable at these times? Can it be tested periodically, and if not, how certain can one be that it will operate effectively on the occasion, which may be far in the future, when it will be needed? Will it be as effective if premises or processes or materials used are changed or modified? Even though it may be 100 per cent effective at controlling accidental losses, could it be put out of action, or by-passed, by someone wishing to cause a deliberate loss? Does it interfere with ease of operations or cause annoyance of any kind to those working near it, so that there is a built-in temptation to prevent it operating? All these questions and many more like them must be asked to obtain a true picture of the effectiveness of any loss control device, be it a sprinkler system, an intruder detection system, a machine guard, or any other.

The number and nature of these questions show the need to look beyond the expert's solution to a loss control problem and to consider the organisational situation into which it is going to be installed, for the psychological aspects of loss control are as important as the physical.

The psychological aspect

On the psychological side, awareness is the key factor. Everyone connected with the organisation must be made aware that losses are possible, and, equally, that they can be controlled. But awareness on its own is not enough. There must also be motivation to take part in the loss control effort. To an extent, this means simply that general management must be good. It means that relations between various levels and various activities within the organisation must be harmonious, so that they do not feel separate and antagonistic towards each other. If they do, then the loss control efforts of one group, however good, can expect no support, and may even be deliberately or inadvertently sabotaged by another.

The resources available

An alternative way of classifying approaches to any kind of loss control is to consider the various types of resources available to the risk manager. These are as follows:

- (*a*) human resources;
- (*b*) physical resources;
- (*c*) organisational resources;
- (*d*) educational resources;
- (*e*) financial resources.

Human resources

Human resources are the first line of defence against any type of loss. Human beings are not nearly so effective as machines at avoiding mistakes, but they are very good at detecting and correcting them, and it is often the immediate intuitive action of someone who happens to be on the spot at the right time that is the difference between a trivial incident and a catastrophic loss.

Everyone in the organisation, therefore, can, and should be, involved in the process of loss control. Managers, foremen, plant operators, engineers, technicians and office staff all have a part to play. All have the ability to identify potential loss and to do something about it, even if that something may only be to think what they are doing and so avoid causing the loss!

Every organisation has a wealth of loss control talents among its own staff, and the risk manager's aim must be to make full use of those talents, individually and in combination, to prevent or reduce loss. Other human resources are available externally, in the form of experts and consultants of all kinds. Technical problems often need technical solutions, and advice on loss control problems frequently will have to be sought outside. Such expertise is valuable, but the involvement of an expert must not be allowed to become an excuse for everyone else to neglect their role in loss control. Risk management is only fully effective if everyone is involved.

Physical resources

The use of physical devices to prevent or to reduce the effect of loss has been discussed earlier in this chapter. When one talks of loss control, it is devices of this kind that first come to mind, but they do not remove the need for human involvement. There is a cynical view that if you try to solve a problem by using a machine, you end up with two problems – the original one and the machine itself. That is the outlook of an extreme pessimist, but it is a useful reminder that, however efficiently a device may be designed to function, there will still be a need for human observation and organisation to ensure that it is kept in a condition to perform when it is needed, and that it remains the appropriate method of loss control in what is unlikely to be a totally unchanging environment.

Organisational resources

Organisational resources are the opportunities open to an enterprise's management to deploy its human loss control resources to the best advantage. The aim should be to make loss control an integral part of the company's normal activities rather than an interruption of them. Much loss prevention publicity is designed to remind people not to do something which might allow a fire to start, result in an accident, permit a theft to take place, or cause some other kind of loss. All too often the action warned about is one that is easily done. It is a sounder policy to design the way things are done in the company so that it is easier to avoid a loss than to cause one. If this is done to the maximum extent, the company will be using the natural tendency to follow the easiest course rather than fighting against it.

Loss control will be helped, too, if the enterprise is so organised that there is every encouragement for all employees to participate in, and to make recommendations and suggestions about, prevention or reduction of losses. This is an important part of the participative nature of effective risk management. Risk cannot be managed by a single risk manager, nor by a risk management department, however large, and enlisting the help of every employee in the control of loss is an important step in making everyone aware of the need to identify a new risk as it arises. Loss control is an excellent starting point, because it does not require anyone to look beyond the activities in which they are themselves involved, and on which they will all feel they are to some extent expert.

Educational resources

Educational resources must be used in conjunction with organisational means to make fullest use of the human power for loss control within the company. Education is an important part of the job of any risk manager, and what he must teach everyone with whom he comes into contact, and encourage them to pass on to everyone else in the company, can be summed up in three propositions, as follows:

1. That risk exists – awareness of risk must be created before risk identification can become part of any job.
2. That something can be done about it – risk awareness can be a negative thing if it leads to excessive risk aversion, or to a fatalistic acceptance of things going wrong.
3. That it is everyone's job to help in identifying and controlling risk.

Financial resources

Financial resources are essential, because loss control, like any other activity in a company, costs money, and will be in competition for funds with other projects which may be more attractive because they offer the positive prospect of additional profit, rather than the negative one of preventing the drain on profitability that loss represents. This always needs to be borne in mind, as a reminder of the need to quantify the benefits of proposed loss control activities when they are proposed. Since their true value will lie in the losses that do not occur, nothing more than an estimate of the benefit side of the cost/benefit calculation will be possible, and a range of values assuming the best case, the worst case and a predictable value usually will provide a better framework for deciding whether or not the expenditure should be incurred.

Commitment

There must be a firm management commitment to the positive control of losses, and this commitment must be effectively communicated, preferably by means of a definite policy statement, which is not a mere form of words, but which is a basis for action and example. The control of losses, while co-ordinated centrally, must be made a clear part of all duties, and each manager, at whatever level in the organisation he may be, made accountable for losses occurring within his sphere of authority. Only in this way can the idea that loss control is everyone's job be communicated throughout the organisation.

Awareness

If the basic commitment is there, loss control can express itself in practical terms in every activity within an organisation. Awareness of the possibility of loss will mean that potential losses will be one of the factors taken into consideration whenever a new activity is planned, or when existing methods are reviewed. It will mean that staff are encouraged to draw attention to any aspects of their own particular job or surroundings which seem to make a loss possible. Toleration of unsafe conditions or the despatch of defective products, for example, will become, and will be expected to become, unacceptable.

Measurement

With better awareness of possible loss comes the opportunity of better measurement, both of the probability and the potential severity of loss, and also of the critical conditions in which losses can come about. This means more reliable figures of possible maximum loss, better information about the adequacy of physical protections against loss, and a more realistic look at the true value to an organisation of any of its activities which entail a particularly high degree of risk.

If awareness of the possibility of loss leads to a proper evaluation of the loss potential and the true cost of controlling loss in a particular high risk activity, it may well be found that the commercial benefit derived from that operation is insufficiently high for its continuance to be justified. All too often the risk manager finds that within his organisation there is one activity, peripheral to the main operations of the organisation, which contributes very little to the organisation's profitability, but which carries a potential for catastrophic loss out of all proportion to its value. As we have seen, proper measurement can also help in determining the level of expenditure on loss prevention measures which is justified by the probability of loss.

Recording and monitoring

As with all aspects of risk management, loss control is a continuous process. The risks that have been countered may change, process or organisational changes may make the loss control programme less effective, and, as its requirements are absorbed into routine, observance of loss control procedures may become lax. Periodical reviews of all loss control systems are essential, in order to check that they are still needed, that they are still the most appropriate response to the particular risk and that they are still working efficiently.

Because it is possible that those within an organisation may be too familiar with it to form an objective view of its loss potential, the loss control effort can be helped by taking advantage of outside services – insurers, brokers and specialists in particular types of protection can all help by making periodic checks, particularly of key locations.

This programme of review can be further backed up by a system under which all incidents which cause, or could cause, loss however small are reported. If these are recorded and analysed, recurrent small losses can be eliminated. Such a system can also give advance warning of the possibility of a catastrophic loss, even if the incident which reveals that possibility is itself trivial.

11. Contingency planning

In the narrower sense in which the term is generally understood, contingency planning forms an important part of loss control. Yet if one interprets it more widely, one could say that the whole of risk management is an exercise in contingency planning. One must first identify the contingencies for which planning is necessary, and then decide on the appropriate action to be taken to prevent them occurring or, if this is not possible, to minimise their adverse effects.

To ask, "What happens if . . .?" must provoke the further question: "What can be done about it?" Clearly prevention is better than cure, but contingency planning (in the more restricted sense) is a recognition of the facts that some things cannot be prevented, and that even where they can, the preventive measures adopted may fail wholly or in part.

It is unwise, however, to lose sight of the contingency planning aspects of all the stages of risk management. Planning which begins with the emergency – fire, flood, escape of toxic materials, denial of access, the need to recall a batch of faulty products or whatever else it may be – and ignores what has happened in the company before that point, runs the risk of being insufficiently related to the individual needs of the company. It may be an excellent plan in general terms, but it may overlook in particular the ways in which the methods adopted to control loss may themselves influence the nature of the emergency and in some circumstances even increase its severity.

The decision to install sprinklers, for example, will introduce a risk of water damage as a side-effect of reducing the risk of fire. Thus the contingency plan for fire must take account of the possible need to dispose of quantities of water-damaged stock over and above that affected by the fire brigade's hoses. But the contingency plan must also recognise that dependence upon an automatic system may make the disaster worse, if it fails, than it would have been if the system had never been installed. Perhaps before the sprinklers were installed there was a periodic patrol of the buildings at night to check that all was well. If the possibility of fire was the main reason for the patrol, it will probably have been discontinued when the sprinklers were fitted. Obviously, the sprinklers are a much better protection, but if the fire started when the sprinkler system was, for some reason, out of commission, the absence of the relatively inefficient older system could make the difference between a minor and a catastrophic loss. Any contingency plan must therefore be flexible enough, or contain sufficient options, to be effective when the loss prevention systems installed do not work as well as when they do.

Phases of contingency planning

Contingency planning must therefore be adequate to cover three phases of activity. These are shown in Fig. 11.1. The first of these phases will be the subject of more detailed treatment in the chapters which follow, and we shall therefore concentrate here on emergency and recovery plans. It is most unlikely that these will be totally separate, because one will naturally merge into the other, and much that is done at the time of the loss will be as much concerned with long-term recovery as with immediate remedies. It is, however, convenient to examine them individually.

Phase	Type of plan	Aims
Pre-loss	Loss prevention	To prevent occurrence of loss
Loss and immediate post-loss period	Emergency plan	To minimise duration and extent of loss To maximise safety of persons and salvage
Post-loss	Recovery plan	To minimise interruption to normal activities

Fig. 11.1   *Phases of contingency planning*

Emergency plans

Action at the time of an emergency must be swift, certain and effective. Some improvisation may very well be necessary to meet the particular circumstances of the emergency, but the main lines of action can be determined in advance, and to have a plan of action ready to be put into effect at a moment's notice will save the most valuable of commodities when disaster strikes – time. Once the emergency has begun, it is too late to begin the necessary pre-planning and training.

The need, in an emergency, is that as many people as possible should know what action to take, when to take it, and, equally important, when to stop. As a very simple example, all staff should know which type of portable fire extinguisher to use on which kind of fire, should know how to operate an extinguisher, if possible having practised with one, and should know at what stage first aid fire extinguishment of this kind should cease and the premises be completely evacuated.

Everyone should know where to go. Recognised reporting centres enable checks to be made that all are accounted for, and also make it easier for staff to be deployed to help in loss limitation efforts. Reporting centres should be selected not only for administrative convenience against a background of normal activity but also with some imagination about what an emergency situation would be like. The routes people are required to take should not run counter to their natural inclinations in a crisis. Research carried out after the Flixborough explosion* into the routes taken by survivors revealed the extent to which they followed their instinctive desire to head for water, and made for the river bordering the site rather than follow the laid down reporting instructions – fortunately for them, as it happened, since the official reporting centre was totally destroyed in the blast.

People should know what assistance to call and how to call it. This will cover the whole range of internal and external assistance, from alerting the company's own security services or works fire brigade to summoning the public emergency services.

Most important, staff must be able to recognise the agreed signals for action. Much time can be lost by people debating whether or not an incident is serious enough for action laid down in an emergency plan to be taken. At the extreme, an excellent emergency plan might never be put into effect because the decision to activate it was delayed too long.

The exact nature of the action in the emergency plan will, of course, vary according to the nature of the emergency, and to the particular vulnerabilities of the individual company, but it may include such matters as follows:

(a) safety of life;
(b) planned evacuation of the premises and possibly of others nearby;
(c) fire extinguishment;
(d) minimising water damage – by placing sandbags, covering machinery with sheets and pumping or other removal of excess water;
(e) restoration of security;
(f) fast, safe plant shut-down;
(g) initiating product recalls.

Priorities for action will often depend upon the trade in which the company operates, but common to all emergency plans will be a need for co-operative effort.

Clearly, specialists will play a big role in foreseeing what action will be

---

*See "Flixborough: The Human Response", K. Westgate (University of Bradford Disaster Research Unit Occasional Paper No. 7), 1975.

necessary, in planning it and in controlling it if the plan has to be put into effect. Those whose job is concerned with the prevention of accidents or losses, such as safety officers, fire prevention officers and quality controllers, will be closely involved, but so, too, will staff whose expertise is less obviously relevant. Engineers, lawyers, marketing and public relations staff may have very important roles to play in the operation of an emergency plan. Co-ordination of all these efforts may present a problem unless the company actively practises risk management, in which case the risk manager, who probably already will be co-ordinating the efforts of these and other members of staff in the identification and reduction of risk, might well be a suitable co-ordinator of the plan.

No one seriously disputes the advantage of having an emergency plan, but many companies find it hard to invest the necessary money and time in drawing one up. Major hazards legislation now requires the preparation of such a plan where hazardous materials are stored in quantity. The arguments for planning to meet disaster in other industries and from other sources are no less strong.

Recovery planning

Stopping the loss as quickly as possible at the minimum possible cost is only part of the contribution of contingency planning. Any emergency introduces an abnormal situation which interrupts the normal flow of a company's business, and there will therefore be a need for a further plan to help the company get back to its normal level of trading as quickly as possible.

In considering a recovery plan, one inevitably moves into the field of speculative risk and top management decisions. Questions such as the extent and nature of competition in the market, the relative contributions of particular products, the effect of seasonal factors and fashion on demand for products, and the possibility of substitute products and alternative formulations may all have to be considered. There can, however, be an important contribution from the pure risk side in the form of the interruption report prepared to assist the underwriter of the company's consequential loss (business interruption) insurance. This will have highlighted many of the potential problems the company might face in getting back to normal after an interruption, and although its horizons will be bounded by its concentration on interruption caused by the perils being insured against, it can form a useful starting point for a recovery plan.

The problems which have to be overcome may be of many kinds, but those most likely to be faced will be the adverse effects upon one's market share or standing if goods cannot be supplied, and unavailability of the various elements necessary for production. If there is difficulty in having materials, plant, premises, labour or transport available when the company is ready to use it, the period of interruption will be prolonged, and the more specialised any of them need to be for the company's purposes, the greater the potential disruption may be.

Surmounting such problems may call for ingenuity, but an ingenious way of obtaining and using alternative materials will be ineffective if it is found that the substitute materials cannot be processed on the alternative replacement plant which a separate ingenious solution has provided.

Co-operation between the various departments concerned in returning the company to normal is therefore essential. Ideally, a recovery plan should be devised at a conference attended by all departmental heads, where each major threat can be considered and possible solutions discussed together. In this way, some at least of the post-loss difficulties can be foreseen and methods of surmounting them discussed. There may be other benefits, since considering hypothetical interruptions may raise the question of whether the normal way of doing things is in fact the best. One of the by-products of such a conference may thus be some suggestions for ways in which the company's efficiency could be improved in normal circumstances.

Such an approach to setting up a recovery plan is costly, and there may be a temptation to think of it as something to be done once only. Nothing stands still, however, least of all risk, and so periodic updating of the plan will be essential.

Common features of emergency and recovery plans

Although the purposes of the two types of plan are different, their three basic constituents are the same – information, responsibilities and practice.

Information

Information is at the heart of both kinds of plan. Without the necessary information, action in an emergency will be undirected and taken on the basis of intuition or guesswork rather than knowledge. Lack of information in the post-loss phase will impose additional delays while it is obtained and verified. An essential part of the planning programme will therefore be to decide what information will be necessary and useful both during and after the emergency, to obtain and check it and to record it in a form which will be accessible when it is needed.

Much of the information will relate to the company's normal way of doing business and will be readily available, but some of it would only be needed in an emergency, and must be obtained specially. It is obviously easier to do that in advance at one's leisure than to attempt to put the information together in the disorganised environment of the emergency.

Typically, it will be necessary to record names, addresses, telephone numbers and names of contacts for all the organisations which may be of help at the time of the emergency or afterwards. In addition to emergency services, the list may include the following:

(a) suppliers of all kinds of temporary and permanent materials and labour that may be needed;

(*b*)   estate agents specialising in the appropriate types of property;

(*c*)   machinery suppliers and hirers;

(*d*)   usual and alternative suppliers of raw materials;

(*e*)   salvage and waste disposal firms;

(*f*)   construction and repair firms.

Compiling the list presupposes some thought as to the possible nature and extent of the emergency and its consequent interruption, so that the more complete the planning exercise, the fuller and more relevant the information will be.

Once compiled, the information must be kept up to date and it must be safeguarded so that it is available instantly when it is needed. A single copy locked in the compiler's desk will not do; it must be distributed widely to all those who may have to use it, and it should preferably be in a form which makes it easy to consult, but difficult to file away and forget.

Responsibilities

Responsibilities for initiating and supervising each stage of the planned action must be spelled out in the plan. This is all part of ensuring that everyone knows what to do when the time comes. There should be sufficient delegation of duties to ensure that senior management are not burdened with unnecessary responsibilities at a time when they are bound to be under severe pressure, and are having to deal with all the unexpected aspects of an emergency which no plan, however full, can cater for.

It is also important to ensure that alternatives are nominated for each responsibility, in order that the plan is not hindered by the fact that the officer responsible for one particular aspect of it is on holiday, on a course, sick, out of the country, visiting another site or absent for any other reason at the time of the emergency, or even that he is one of its victims. The plan must designate clearly the persons who have the authority to put it into effect. No company wants to set a full-scale emergency plan in action every time there is a fire in a waste-paper basket, but, equally, it wants to be certain that the plan will operate when circumstances warrant it. The person who is to take the decision, and his deputies who are authorised to take it in his absence, must be identified in the plan, and their identities must be known to all those responsible for particular aspects of the plan.

Practice

Practice is the third important feature. Only by testing parts of the plan in simulated emergencies can weaknesses in it be rectified before it has to be put into effect in earnest. Like risk management itself, perfecting a plan can be represented as a management decision making loop. The first stage is to identify the problem. Next a plan to counter the problem is devised, recorded and communicated to all those who have a part to play in it. The next stage is to test it, to monitor the test results and amend the plan in the light of the lessons learned.

It will never be easy to arrange a full-scale rehearsal for disaster, except in particularly hazardous industries, where local emergency services may themselves wish to organise a training exercise simulating a disaster at the plant, but if such an exercise can be staged, much can be learned about the company itself and its organisation, as well as about the contingency plan and its shortcomings.

Where full-scale practice is not possible, one may still be able to test parts of the plan. Even a simple fire drill is a beginning. It may be possible to graft on to that simple evacuation exercise some special features which will test some other aspects of the plan at the same time. Undoubtedly, the more that can be practised the better, especially if doing so helps to increase the general awareness of risk and the realisation that something can be done about it, and that it is part of everyone's job to help in doing it. That, of course, is the main message of risk management in a nutshell.

12. The protection of property

The importance of loss control in a risk management programme was explained in general terms in Chapter 10, but how it is to be put into practice will differ both according to the aspect of the organisation that is to be protected and the types of losses it must be protected against.

The first main feature of the organisation we will consider is its property. As always in risk management, the first essential is to identify exactly what is at risk and what threatens it; in other words, one must apply in detail the consideration of the various components of risk – resources, threats, modifying factors and consequences – which were discussed in Chapter 4.

Types of property

The types of resources that are included under the general heading of "property" are very varied and each will be potentially subject to a different range of threats. In broad terms, we can classify property under the following headings:

(a) fixed property
    e.g. land,
        buildings,
        services,
        fixtures and fittings,
        plant and fixed equipment;
(b) moveable property
    e.g. portable equipment,
        stock,
        vehicles,
        documents;
(c) money and its equivalents;
(d) non-tangible forms of property
    e.g. rights and know-how,
        commercial secrets.

Types of threat

Next we must consider the different threats to property. The first division that suggests itself is between natural perils and those which are man-made. But as soon as one lists the elemental threats – earthquakes, volcanic perils, wind, water, fire and explosion – one can see that, although nature may supply the force, the consequences can be substantially modified by human actions. Construction, siting and protections may increase or decrease the importance of these natural forces as perils and some, especially fire and explosion, may deliberately be brought about by the hand of man.

It is probably more appropriate, therefore, to follow this line of thought and to classify threats by two main divisions – the accidental and the deliberate – while recognising that the same active force may appear in both sections, according to whether it is directed by man or not.

The categories will therefore look like this:

Accidental	*Deliberate*
Earthquake	Damage, destruction, removal,
Volcanic eruption	deprivation of use
Windstorm	– by human force or action
Natural water perils	– by deliberate use of natural
Natural and accidental fire	forces, e.g. arson
Lightning	– by dishonesty
Accidental explosion	

As a cross-check, one can then analyse the "deliberate" threats, according to the possible motives involved. These will include:

(*a*) gain
    e.g. theft,
        fraud;
(*b*) political or social reasons
    e.g. war,
        sabotage,
        actions of strikers;
(*c*) revenge or dissatisfaction
    e.g. malicious damage,
        arson;
(*d*) destructive urges
    e.g. vandalism.

The distinction between accidental and deliberate threats is an important one in considering the protection of property. This is because the type of preventive measures necessary will not be the same if the need is merely to protect against an undirected force, as if the threat includes the possibility of the protective devices or systems being outwitted or rendered ineffective either before or during the occurrence that produces the loss.

This highlights the importance of not relying on physical protective measures only, if there is a possibility of a "deliberate" aspect to the threat. Such precautions must be backed up by organisational systems to ensure that they will continue to operate when they are needed. At the same time it must be recognised that it is possible, given the necessary time and opportunity, for men to find a way to defeat any man-made system.

Cross-checking

The next stage is to check each item of property against the list of threats to identify the vulnerabilities which call for protection. Not only will the major threats be different for different types of property, but they will also be different for the same kinds of property in different industries. Land, for example, will be thought of in most companies as being most unlikely to suffer any continuing damage or loss from the perils we have listed. Whatever happens, it is likely to retain its value. With agriculture or the extractive industries, however, land may essentially be the business itself, so that efforts to protect it become vital and may merit the spending of large sums of money.

Buildings and services are more likely to be affected by perils which will destroy or damage them, but as soon as one considers other kinds of fixed and moveable property the risk of dishonesty must also be taken into account. As one moves on to money and non-tangible property, dishonesty in one form or another becomes the major risk to be protected against.

Types of protection

Once this analysis had been made, it is possible to determine the method of protection that is most appropriate for each item of property. It must be accepted that it will never be possible to achieve perfect protection for every piece of property – economic considerations must always be borne in mind – and there will inevitably be cases where the ideal protection for one item of property may reduce the protection for another associated with it or even create new risks for it, as, for example, when a sprinkler system which will reduce the risk of damage by fire to a building and most of its contents may introduce an additional major hazard for one small part of the contents which is abnormally susceptible to water damage, or even to changes in humidity.

There are three main methods of property protection to be considered:

(*a*) reduction of vulnerability;
(*b*) physical protection systems;
(*c*) organisational systems;

and in most cases it will be found that a combination of the three methods is necessary.

Reduction of vulnerability

The range of hazards we have been discussing are largely external to the company and once a decision has been taken that certain property shall be located in a particular place, the opportunities for avoiding the hazards entirely are greatly reduced. Nevertheless it is usually possible, provided one has correctly identified the vulnerabilities, to reduce them. Features of construction are likely to play a big part in this approach to property protection.

Appropriate fire separation can be provided within and between buildings, while a construction appropriate to the weather extremes that may be expected will avoid having flat roofs if there is a possibility of them collapsing under a weight of snow, for example, or avoid storing, say, finished steel products at a point on a site where the contours will ensure that they are in the path of surface water if there is a cloud-burst. In reducing vulnerability to natural perils in this way, it is always wise to plan for conditions worse than those ever recorded locally. Systematic weather recording has only been going on for a very brief period of the earth's history and climatic variations may always be greater than one expects.

There may have been changes which render the experience of the past unreliable as a guide to the future. Extensive development may, for example, have taken place, so that areas of open land have been surfaced and built on. With less open ground to absorb rainfall, it may not need anything like the worst recorded storm locally to produce a flood.

This approach to protection is, of course, not limited to natural perils. Good housekeeping will reduce property losses of all kinds within the company's premises, while proper attention to maintenance, packaging and methods of storage will often show that even some damage to plant, products and other materials which is accepted as inevitable can in fact be reduced.

Physical protection systems

Whereas the aim in reducing vulnerability has generally been to minimise the likelihood of the risk occurring and is thus mainly concerned with the pre-loss phase, physical protection systems are designed to reduce the effect of the loss as it occurs.

Into this category come such devices as sprinklers, explosion suppression devices, intruder alarms and security devices of all kinds. Many of these will be designed to work automatically and it is essential to develop means of testing that they will be effective. Attention must be paid to periods when they may be out of service for repair, maintenance, or through the interruption of public services on which they depend, so that, whenever possible, some alternative safeguard is introduced then.

Above all, it must be remembered that such devices are themselves a form of property which need to be protected, both from "accidental" and "deliberate" perils. The more vital the property they protect, the more important it becomes that they should themselves be properly protected.

Organisational systems

Physical protection must be backed up by organisational systems, not only to monitor and ensure their effectiveness, but also to supplement them by preparing those concerned for the possibility of loss or damage, so that when it occurs as little time as possible is spent in stopping it. Since it is important that everyone should know what action should be taken in the event of any kind of foreseeable loss, emergency plans, which were discussed in the last chapter, can be vital to effective loss control. It is also desirable that there should be a regular system of loss and incident reporting to provide information on which future action to control losses or necessary modifications to existing systems may be based.

The essential here is to create a system which enables one to count the number of occurrences of a particular type (including, wherever possible, the "near misses", where the necessary circumstances for a loss came into being, but where, as it happened, no damage was caused), to measure their severity, to classify them both as to cause and effect, and to use this information to audit the effectiveness of the property protection programme. Organisational systems as a means of property protection are accepted as normal practice in the accounting field, and a company should be prepared to extend the concept to an audit of its systems for preventing loss by causes other than dishonesty.

The regular provision of information and the analysis of that information for the light shed upon the company's successes and failures in protecting its property in all its varied forms can be a most useful tool in improving its loss control. It will, of course, be evident that such a system can also provide some valuable information for decisions about the appropriate method of financing a particular risk.

13. The protection of earnings

The survival of any commercial organisation depends upon a continuing stream of earnings, and creation and maintenance of that stream of earnings is a fundamental activity in any business. When potential threats to the organisation are being considered, however, it is very easy for attention to be concentrated on the threats of material loss or damage, particularly if a possible catastrophe is concerned, and for too little thought to be given to the ways in which the flow of earnings may be interrupted. This is particularly dangerous, since a comparatively small amount of damage may lead to a serious interruption in earnings, and in some circumstances earnings may be lost with no related material loss at all.

If, for example, it is suggested that something in one of the company's products is toxic or may cause cancer, or if there are similar suspicions about the products of other firms in the same industry, it may be necessary to stop production, to withdraw or reformulate the product, even though the suspicions may later be proved to have been unfounded.

Importance of protection

Protection of future earnings becomes even more important because risk financing can be of only temporary help in this type of loss. The lost earnings may be replaced by insurance for a limited period, but there must always come a day when no further insurance benefit is payable. When that happens, there may still be a loss of earnings to be faced.

Reliance on insurance as a method of financing earnings loss can also be unwise where presence in the market is of crucial importance to the company. The indemnity period under an insurance policy may be measured in years, but what consolation is that to a company which would suffer an irreparable loss of earnings if its product disappeared from the market for a matter of months only? Customers might be lost to competitors offering similar products, or an alternative technology may be adopted by leading users as a consequence of the period of absence from the market, which may mean that the market is irretrievably lost.

The emphasis must therefore be on protection to minimise the probability of the loss occurring, and on drawing up contingency plans to

72

ensure that if there should be an occurrence which threatens a serious loss of earnings, a programme of necessary measures to minimise the loss and to safeguard the company's market presence would be ready to put into action at once. In talking of earnings, of course, we do not refer to profit alone, for a stoppage may cause the loss of more than just profit – a lack of turnover may prevent overheads being recovered in full.

Since applying risk management to the problem of threats to continued earnings is very much a matter of deciding on and implementing the best possible forms of protection against loss, it will be of particular importance that the vital flows of earnings and the potential threats to them are correctly identified.

Identifying earnings sources

Identification of the main sources of earnings should not be difficult, but care will be necessary to identify any points in the supply, production and distribution chain where the flow of earnings is dependent upon the uninterrupted function of a particular operation which is inadequately protected. Flow charts can be particularly helpful in identifying such points. Protection in this case may either be physical, or consist of alternative methods of carrying out the operations which are either in existence or which can be called on at short notice if required. The range of possible measures is endless, for it will vary with the type of business and the way in which earnings can be interrupted. Sprinklers, stand-by plant or power sources, buffer stocks, provisional arrangements with alternative suppliers, or alternative product formulations, may each be the answer to a specific problem of safeguarding continuing earnings.

Identifying threats to earnings

Identification of potential threats to earnings requires a much wider view than is the case with the identification of threats to property. It includes, of course, consideration of many of those threats to property, for earnings may well be dependent upon the continuing existence of certain property and the measures outlined in Chapter 12 for the protection of property will also take care of the potential loss of earnings.

Threats to earning capacity must also be identified and they may well be less obvious than major threats to property. They may well involve property but there may be no obvious relationship between the importance of a piece of property as property and its importance to the flow of earnings. A machine or building may be of low value and possibly overlooked when property threats are being considered. At the same time, its importance for the earnings of the business may be enormous.

Threats to people

The key threat may not be to a machine or a building, but to a person. There is a tendency for most specialists not to transmit to others, or to commit to any form of record, knowledge about their activity which may be vital to its continuance. This is particularly so where the knowledge consists of how to cope with abnormal situations. The possibility of an interruption in earnings if that knowledge is not there may easily be overlooked. One meets companies whose only contingency plan is to rely on the ingenuity, organising skill and contacts of one prominent individual in the company. This is particularly the case with some small but successful companies which have been built up through the entrepreneurial talents and drive of one man. The possibility that he may be among the victims of the incident which calls for his special knowledge and skill is not considered.

Threats to records

Wherever possible, therefore, knowledge must be recorded, but this can itself present problems. To be dependent on records means that the records must themselves be protected or duplicated elsewhere. While this may be an excellent protection against threats which are accidental in origin, it may easily increase threats which are deliberately brought about – the more information which is available and the more it is duplicated, the greater is the chance that wrongful use may be made of it.

This is particularly the case if computers are used as the record store. Not only does dependence upon computers tend to concentrate the risk of interruption through lack of access to records, but this dependence may often be accentuated because of the need to rely on a small number of computer-trained individuals to provide the link needed to record, amend or obtain information. Computer staff may themselves be among the specialists we have mentioned earlier who are inclined to keep to themselves knowledge which may be vital to the continued earnings of the organisation.

External threats

Threats to earnings are not confined to areas within the company's direct control. The continued willingness of customers to purchase the company's products and the continuation of vital supplies to the company are as important to the preservation of earnings as anything that happens on the company's own premises.

Loss, damage or interruption of business suffered by a customer may prevent him purchasing the company's products in his usual quantities or at all, and if a significant proportion of a company's earnings depends upon those sales, the effect of the incident may be more serious for the company than for the customer to whom it happened. Similarly, misfortune may strike at suppliers, and again the effect of the loss may be felt most seriously by the company deprived of these supplies. Supplies can be of many kinds – raw materials, equipment, components, consumable stores can all be essential for the continued flow of earnings. Nor must one overlook power and water supplies and, in some industries, waste disposal services.

Types of threat

A wide range of possible threats has been discussed in connection with the protection of property and all these threats must also be regarded as potential causes of loss of earnings. One must, however, also consider a range of threats to earnings which would not necessarily involve property loss or damage. It is important here not to confine one's consideration to threats which are insurable. Stoppage for any reason could mean a loss of earnings, and the effect would be the same whether the stoppage were from a cause which might be considered an "insurable" risk or from one in the field of what is conventionally considered "commercial risk".

Interruption of supplies, processes or deliveries must be foreseen as far as possible. Causes such as strikes, occupation of premises by employees, boycott of products and even precautionary evacuation if one's own or neighbouring premises store or use particularly hazardous materials should all be included in the study.

Methods of protection

Only by meticulous analysis of the range of potential threats can adequate protection of earnings be devised. The protections designed to prevent property loss will minimise earnings loss, provided, of course, that they do not themselves introduce new systems on which the continuance of the business is dependent, and thus introduce new threats to earnings. Modification of methods of operation to eliminate vulnerabilities wherever possible and realistic contingency planning to minimise the effects of those threats which cannot be removed in this way will be the form that most effective earnings protection will take.

Current trends

The vulnerability of earnings becomes greater as modern trends alter the way business is carried on. The tendency towards increased concentration, for example, poses a growing threat to earnings. Production has increasingly become concentrated in single plants, which may in the extreme case become the sole production source for a whole country, or even a whole continent. The vulnerability, not only of the producing company, but of its customers, and perhaps even of their customers, can only be vastly increased in these circumstances. The economies of scale can only be purchased at the expense of a corresponding increase in risk, which ought to be considered when, say, a single large distribution warehouse is built to replace a number of smaller, scattered ones. The vulnerability factor in the cost–benefit calculation may too often be overlooked.

There is also a tendency for the profitability of a plant to depend upon a very high volume of output, which increases the vulnerability of the earnings from that plant, not by introducing new threats, but by reducing the margin before the operation of a threat produces an adverse result.

As machinery and processes, too, become more specialised, so the possibilities of finding alternatives in the event of interruption are seriously diminished.

At the same time that production is becoming concentrated, the power to interrupt production appears to be becoming more widely disseminated. Deliberately caused losses comprise an increasing proportion of the total number of losses; action for political ends and in support of social aims is being more accurately directed at vulnerable points in the industrial and commercial world. At the same time, nations which are sole or major suppliers of important raw materials are discovering and using their powers over user nations.

It is against this background that effective protections against loss of earnings must be evolved. The threats to earnings may be much more varied and more difficult to identify and counter than the threats to property, but their potential to bring disaster upon the company is likely to be greater. They cannot therefore be ignored and a programme of risk management that does not make the best attempt possible at meeting threats to earnings can never be anything like complete.

14. The protection of vital records

The more complex a business becomes, the more it depends upon its records. What it is making, or plans to make, what services it is supplying, exactly how the work is done, who its suppliers and its existing and prospective customers are, who owes it money and what it owns – all this information and more is necessary for the continuance of the business and has to be recorded. Such records must necessarily be available for day-to-day reference, but unless they are adequately duplicated or protected, the company will run the risk, if a disaster strikes, of losing not only its physical assets, but also the records which would provide its only means of reconstructing the business.

Some companies recognise this fully – even, like some of the largest US-based international companies, going to the lengths of storing away the records necessary to prove their corporate title in vaults deep underground where they will be safe even in the event of nuclear disaster. All too often, however, vital information is not adequately recorded, or, if it is, is insufficiently protected, not just against fortuitous loss, but against the ever-increasing threat of criminal abstraction or misuse. This latter will be more fully covered in Chapter 15, and we will here confine our consideration to accidental loss, without, at this stage, discussing the situation where protections are deliberately avoided or rendered inoperative.

Identifying vital records

The identification of records which are either valuable to a business, or vital to the continuance of its operations is a task which is probably given insufficient attention in most companies. It is essentially a task which calls for a central overview, for every department in a company will have its own ideas as to which records are vital. The tendency will be for each department to identify those records which enable it to do its work easily, or in the way it does it at present, rather than those which enable it to function at all. Furthermore, the total of "vital" documents identified by a department-by-department enquiry will almost certainly be far greater than can economically be protected.

A clear, central view of which operations must continue if the company is to survive and which records are vital to their continuance is essential in the identification stage. A check list is often used, which covers the obvious items such as debtor records and share certificates for example. But there are dangers in relying on a check list which has not been drawn up with the company itself specifically in mind. Every company will have a different list of records on which its uninterrupted operations depend, or which could only be replaced at great expense if, indeed, they could be replaced at all. In some companies, a loss of records can mean that very many man-hours of work, and the money that is represented by that work, have been wasted. This could be the case with long-term research, for example, or with the development of a complicated computer programme.

The key to identifying vital records is to ask the question which we have seen is basic to all risk management investigations: "What happens if . . .?" Each type of record should be checked to see if the business could function effectively without it. If not, a check should be made to see whether it is duplicated elsewhere. Where there is such duplication, it is important to distinguish between cases where this is the consequence of a formal system, and where it happens by chance.

As well as considering the records necessary for the day-to-day running of the business, it is wise to think of the possibility of certain records being necessary in special circumstances. With the development of products liability law, quality control records are becoming increasingly important as evidence, yet they may well be inadequately protected even in companies alive to the threat of records loss.

Problems of records loss

If records are lost or destroyed, it is often very difficult to know exactly what has been lost until a problem arises the solution of which depends upon using, or referring to, a particular record which is then found to be missing. The problems of records loss are much more difficult to foresee than those of the loss of other types of property loss. If, for example, a building burns down, some idea of the extent of the problem can be obtained immediately by looking at the damage. Loss of records, on the other hand, presents an enormous range of possible implications. The true extent of the threat may remain indeterminable for a long time. If production is interrupted by a property loss, then normal activity is suspended while ways of alleviating the situation are decided on and put into effect. If records are lost, however, administrative demands continue, and there may be no such breathing space.

For a service organisation which is heavily dependent upon its records, the threat to them may be its major vulnerability. If such a company's premises suffer a major fire, it can continue to offer its services almost uninterrupted, except for the delay involved in finding somewhere for its staff to work, provided the records are intact inside fireproof cabinets or are readily reproducible from elsewhere. Without all these pieces of paper, it may be lost.

Forms of protection

It is tempting to see the provision of some form of fire-resistant storage as the answer to the most probable forms of records loss. For some types of record, fire-resistant cabinets can be extremely expensive, particularly for large quantities of plans.

Duplication may prove to be a more satisfactory solution, although one must always remember that if the information is confidential, every extra copy made reduces security. Microfilming may be the answer if the bulk of records is large, or even regular photocopying, with the copies distributed consistently over several dispersed buildings, so that even if a whole building is lost, most of the records will still be available.

Records in use will need to be stored near their users, but there is no need for the duplicates to be anywhere nearby. When planning a dispersal programme, the Flixborough explosion provides a salutary warning. There, the control room and the office, the obvious places to store important records, were both destroyed.

Computerised records

The importance of duplication of information as a means of protection is more often appreciated where systems have been computerised, but it is still necessary to ensure that the duplication is adequate in each particular case. Where mainframe computers are heavily involved in administration work, the centralisation of information means that records can often be far more easily protected than they were in the days of manual operations. Large amounts of information are now concentrated in small quantities of magnetic tape or discs.

This, of course, increases the importance to the company of ensuring that these records are properly backed-up with duplicates which are kept up-dated and properly protected; but if this is done and regularly checked then the records protection problem becomes much smaller. The duplication system must be a formal one, although even with computer records, an informal duplication system may exist. One company which lost 80 per cent of its business records through failure to protect data processing information is reputed to have found that it was in fact able to reinstate most of them over a period of several months from copies of print-outs and other documentation found in the homes and cars of employees. No company would want to be in the position of having to rely on such an unreliable and time-consuming way of getting back into business. Protection by proper organisation is simpler, more certain, and probably cheaper.

The introduction of personal computers may, however, reintroduce decentralisation of record keeping to individual departments. Systems which stand alone and are not linked into a company network present the same problems as paper records maintained by a single department.

Standards of records protection may vary widely, and it will be necessary to ensure that any records on which the company depends which are stored in this way are properly safeguarded.

The hazard to be countered is not only that of fire. Concentration of records means that, not only is the risk of sabotage of records increased, but also that of total loss by such causes as explosion or damage by aircraft. The latter risk illustrates that it is not necessarily enough to think in terms of strongrooms, fire-resistant storage, or even duplication, if there is insufficient separation between originals and duplicates. When thinking of storage for back-up files, the separation should be measured in miles rather than yards.

Records in process

When records reach their final form, protection can be reduced to simple rules. Information exists, however, and is used before it reaches that final stage. It may be far more difficult to provide adequate protection for, say, unprocessed batches of invoices, or the multitude of rough notes which may be the basis of a major research discovery. It may present a real problem to ensure that such fragmentary records, whose true importance it may be impossible to evaluate accurately at the time they are made, are gathered up overnight and protected or duplicated, but anything that can be done to reduce the risk should be done. Even to ensure that they are placed in a locked desk drawer will provide at least some minor measure of protection against most fires – one company, at least, requires staff to spend the period between a warning alarm and an evacuation alarm in locking away the papers on their desks and in closing windows.

Reliance on records

The greater the complexity of technology and business becomes, the greater dependence there will have to be on records. Fragmentation of a business operation into a number of separate but interdependent specialist areas makes it impossible for any one group of men to be in possession of all the information necessary for the functioning of the business as a whole. Information has to be passed from one part of the organisation to another, and, for efficiency, it tends to take a permanent form. Thus, the information flow takes on a physical form and the company which is dependent upon the passage of information becomes dependent upon the continued existence and availability of the physical records which embody the information.

Records are a kind of property which call for special protection because they are much more likely to be irreplaceable than other kinds, and because they may be the key to replacing other property which has been damaged or lost more quickly, more accurately or more economically. Records embody the history of a company and chart what it is doing at present, but if they are lost, the company may find that with them it has lost its future.

15. The threat of crime

Fortuitous and deliberately caused loss

Protection against fortuitous risks may require solutions of great technical and organisational ingenuity. One can at least feel confident, however, that once the problem has been solved and a suitable and effective system set up then, as long as the system is kept in working order, it will continue to fulfil its function, because the loss-producing force it is designed to counter will remain the same.

When it comes to protection against deliberate acts, however, this assumption can no longer be made, because the effective force in this case is man-directed and can therefore be modified to overcome the protective system. Indeed, the more elaborate the protections that are set up, the greater may be the challenge to some people to find a way of overcoming them, so that the very existence of the protections may in some cases provoke an attack on them. This emphasises the need for constant monitoring of all loss-prevention systems. But, where they are designed to counter the threat of crime, the monitoring must not only check that the systems are still operating correctly, but also review the need for them to be changed.

Crime is a threat which does not only express itself as theft. It can also use a range of effective forces – fire and explosion being of particular importance – to bring about loss or damage. Threats may also be used. Manufacturers and retailers may find themselves faced with extortion based on the actual or alleged contamination or poisoning of goods. Gain is a common motive for loss brought about by criminal means, but it is by no means the only one – revenge, political or social protest, or mere pleasure in destruction, can all result in producing significant losses.

Opportunity crime

We can, however, distinguish two types of crime, which we may call "opportunity" crime and "organised" crime. Opportunity crime is generally on a small scale and its existence and extent can be a measure of the effectiveness of the protections employed, since it is relatively easily deterred. Minor shoplifting, pilferage and acts of vandalism all come into this category, and a good protective system is usually a sufficient defence.

It is often thought, however, that the cost of effective protection is not warranted by the amount of loss sustained. While this economic trade-off must be borne in mind in setting up any kind of loss control system, it should not be forgotten that if a certain level of loss is considered acceptable, and is built into budgets, then it is certain that that level will be attained every year. In many cases, a substantial reduction in the level of tolerated loss could be achieved by relatively simple precautions. In risk management terms, however, losses of this kind are generally of minor importance, because the main emphasis must always be on those losses which could seriously affect the continued existence of the business. One must nevertheless be conscious of the possibility of a major loss being caused by the accumulation of a large number of small losses.

Opportunity crime may assume major proportions when the motivating force is not gain but a desire to destroy. A disgruntled employee or ex-employee may start a fire, for example, which results in extensive and possibly catastrophic loss. Protective systems must take the existence of this type of crime into account, and also allow for the fact that the circumstances in which the loss is caused may be very different from those of normal operations on the premises. Conditions may have been modified to increase the extent of the damage and automatic protections, such as sprinklers, may have been deliberately put out of action.

Organised crime

A similar pattern can be seen with some forms of organised crime – explosions caused by political extremists, for instance. In general, however, organised crime is likely to be carried out for purposes of gain and is likely to present a more serious risk control problem, even though its frequency may be less.

Organised crime can operate on a very large scale, and may be carried out on lines which make it a criminal counterpart of the orthodox business world. It is, moreover, a business with a growth rate which is far in advance of most legitimate enterprises. Like them, organised crime will tend to balance the investment in the enterprise, and the return which can be expected from it, against the risks involved. The organisation may range from one man to a nation-wide conspiracy, but whatever its size, it is likely to be looking for a high return.

Its attention is likely to be directed chiefly to cash and to assets which can be easily moved and easily disposed of to a ready market. Effective protection against this kind of loss will begin with a thorough analysis of the business to identify those things it owns or uses which may be attractive to the criminal. On this analysis will depend the decisions about appropriate methods of protection, whether these be systems of surveillance, physical checks or protective devices of other kinds.

Protecting information

It is not only tangible items of value that are targets for organised crime – information and trade secrets of all kinds are increasingly at risk from those who know they can get a price for them. At one time information could be protected very much as if it were cash, but with the increasing use of EDP (electronic data processing) systems for information storage and retrieval, there is less and less chance of general management knowing which are likely to be the most effective methods of protection, and how unauthorised access to data can be prevented.

Wherever important information is involved, it is wise to set up a system of access to that information based on a strict "need to know" principle, so that access to the whole information is restricted to the absolute minimum number of people, with, in general, only the part that is relevant to his needs being available to any one person.

Refraining from advertising the existence of vital information is a sound basic protection. To publicise the dependence of the company on any particular information flow, directly or by implication, is to increase the risk of an organised attempt to obtain it by unauthorised persons. Similarly, to give publicity to the location where what may be presumed to be important information is processed, is likely to increase the chance of a malicious attack on it by persons ill-disposed towards the company. There is usually no need, for example, to label a computer facility prominently. The company may be proud of it, but the more it is highlighted, the more direct the invitation to damage it.

Separation of risk

In countering all forms of criminal loss, the principle of separation of risk is as important as it is in control of fortuitous loss. Limiting the amount of valuable items held in any one place will increase the time that has to be spent by the criminal and the inconvenience caused to him in bringing about a significant loss, and this may of itself be a deterrent. Even if a loss still occurs, the probability of it reaching large proportions will be greatly reduced.

In the same way, spreading information over several locations or in several unrelated systems will diminish the chances of a catastrophic loss. Centralisation is often operationally more efficient and economic, but it carries with it the penalty of increased vulnerability, which should be included in the cost–benefit calculation.

Security

Security systems are of two types – those which control people, and those which control objects, and it could be argued that the latter are only necessary to the extent that the former fail. Much criminal loss is brought about by, or with the assistance of, persons who are legitimately on the premises, so that security systems must begin with the system for checking the background of new employees, which must be appropriate to the access they will have to key parts of the organisation, valuable materials and vital systems. Discreet checking may be necessary on individual employees, but this must be carried out with extreme care, for the mere knowledge that there is a system for doing so may stir up disaffection which may itself bring about a loss which would not otherwise have occurred.

Physical systems, which restrict access to particular areas or alarms which warn of the presence of intruders, organisational systems which hold safeguards and systems which check into the way operations are carried out, must be regularly tested for efficiency. It should never be forgotten that all these systems ultimately depend on people, who may be more easily subverted or more fallible than the system itself.

Computer fraud

The extensive use of computers has resulted in a number of large-scale frauds in which misuse of the computer has been a prominent ingredient. For the most part, such frauds have not been new in kind, but have rather been the same types of frauds which have long been encountered with manual systems. Computers have, however, often rendered them less easily detectable, for there has been a time lag between the adoption of computerised systems and the adaptation to them of traditional audit methods.

The trend towards transferring data without intervening paper work increases the difficulty of an independent check of the data being processed. The establishment of computer networks may make it difficult for the non-expert to be certain who has legitimate access to information, and impossible for him to detect unauthorised access. In many cases, the imbalance of technical expertise between those responsible for the computer systems and those who seek to check what the computer is doing is so great that the expert's word is accepted with very little question. It is, however, unfortunately the case that the intricacy of modern systems acts as a challenge to some types of computer men to see how they can defeat the system, or turn it to their own advantage.

On-line systems are vulnerable not only to internal manipulation, which should be countered by separation of the various computer functions and good control of access, but also to external interference. This calls for constant vigilance to ensure that, for example, only authorised terminals can gain access to the system. The computer "hacker" entering the system may bear no ill will to the organisation, and have no intention of harming it, but the effects of such unauthorised entry to the system could be very serious. Even if nothing has apparently been tampered with, the fact that unauthorised entry is possible may cast doubts upon the validity of the information stored. If one unauthorised entry is detected, one can only wonder whether there have been others which have remained undetected. What the hacker can do for the sheer enjoyment of defeating a system designed to exclude him, others may have done for gain, or to cause disruption.

Political crime

Political risks add a new dimension to the threat that crime poses. Where damage is caused for political ends, there is likely to be less restraint about how it is brought about, since the aim will be to cause the maximum loss, while there is likely to be less concern for the physical safety of persons on or around the premises. In general, the risk of crime threatens property rather than people, for although injury may be caused incidentally, it is very rarely the intention that this should be so in opportunity crime or in organised crime for gain. When the motives are political, however, the threat to a company may be concentrated in the kidnapping of a top executive, or in a direct threat to the lives of employees by a bomb or of customers by the poisoning of stocks.

Faced with this type of threat, the first essential in loss control is to be aware of the situation in which the business is operating – political risk management is as much about the safety of one's factory or home as it is about a new project in a far distant country. Only if one is aware of the possibility of a politically inspired or a socially inspired threat, and is prepared to take it seriously, can any proper loss control be practised. Defensive measures should be installed to protect the most vulnerable features of the property and appropriate surveillance arranged. However, it may well be found that in these cases the best defence will be a properly drawn-up and adequately practised contingency plan. If these are ready, even if the control devices are overwhelmed, the loss may still be restricted to a level which permits the survival of the enterprise.

16. Health and safety at work

Attitudes towards occupational health and safety in the developed, industrialised nations have followed the same pattern of change from a situation where responsibility for avoiding injury at work rested almost entirely with the employee, to one where the onus is now very much upon the employer to provide safe conditions of work.

The pattern of legislation

In the course of this evolution of attitudes, occupational safety has been the subject of an increasing amount of legislation and has become a specialisation of its own, with an extensive literature. So well established has this specialisation become that it is not always seen as an agent of loss control within the broader framework of risk management. Yet that is what it is and it is unfortunate that safety activities are often seen as a way of complying with legislative requirements, rather than as a part of a wider effort to reduce the effect of risk.

Accident prevention as part of loss control

The prevention of accidents can, however, be looked on in exactly the same light as any other risk reduction effort – it is a way of protecting the assets of the company, here represented by the value of the skills of those who work for it, against forces which will tend to destroy them and so involve the company in loss. Losses stemming from accidents at work consist of far more than the direct costs incurred in treating and compensating the person injured, and the lost value of his services until he returns to work or is replaced. An accident is an interruption in work and time will be lost not only while the injured employee is treated, but also in discussing the accident, and later in investigating the accident, negotiating compensation and possibly in court appearances, if litigation results.

More seriously, an accident may bring to light an unsafe system, or unsafe premises, which may mean that work has to be suspended, either because of legislative compulsion or because workers will not tolerate the conditions, until the defect has been rectified. If the accident involves the release of a pollutant, or if a worker contracts a disease connected with the working environment, pressure from those living near the premises may lead to suspension of operations, with consequent loss to the company.

There is thus a strong financial, as well as a social and humanitariañ incentive for a company to devote a substantial amount of attention to loss control of this kind, and to go beyond simply doing enough to comply with the law.

The accident ratio studies of Heinrich in 1931 and Bird in 1969 have pointed to the correlation between the number of accidents of different degrees of severity. Bird, using a sample of 1.7 million reported accidents, found that for every serious accident there were ten minor injuries, thirty accidents involving property damage and six hundred "near misses", where neither damage nor injury was caused.

This information can be useful in deciding loss control priorities. There is an understandable tendency to concentrate efforts upon preventing a repetition of the last serious accident, irrespective of how improbable it may be that the exact circumstances which caused it will be repeated. It is surely better to use the much more plentiful evidence of probable threats to health and safety which is to be derived from the much more frequent near misses. Study of that data may suggest ways in which major improvements in safety can be made. If, by acting on that information, the number of near misses can be reduced, that in itself can be expected to reduce the number of more serious accidents.

Safety reviews and risk management

It is not always appreciated that a review of a company's activities designed to reduce the possibility of industrial accidents and disease can be a very good starting point for a full risk management review. One has only to draw up a generalised list of the possible sources of injury to employees to see that it is, to a very large extent, also a list of some of the main threats to the company itself. Industrial accidents are not something separate from the material or financial losses that a company may suffer. Accidents which involve damage to property all too often involve personal injury, or an accident to an employee may lead to consequent damage, and both situations may lead to a loss of earnings for the company. A reduction of any type of loss will thus reduce the possibility of the other occurring.

Let us look at some of the features that a health and safety review would cover, and it will become apparent how loss and damage of all kinds are interlinked.

Fire, explosion and hazardous materials

First, one would review the hazard of fire, which takes its toll of life as well as of property. The review would consider the extent and nature of combustible construction materials and contents of premises, the possible sources of ignition, and the devices and construction features which would help or hinder fire-fighting and evacuation of the premises. With this review one would also consider the possibility of explosion, assessing the materials handled, the processes employed and the protective devices installed, and also the general risk presented by hazardous materials of all kinds, whether they be flammable, corrosive or toxic. How they are stored, handled and used in the various processes would be studied, and also the systems and devices used to prevent the accumulation of harmful vapours.

Water perils

Next, one might go on to review the dangers connected with the risks of flood and water damage, to ensure that employees would not be put in danger by a possible inrush of water from any source. One would also consider the effect of water on the materials to be found in the premises to ensure that this would not involve a health risk, and check that electrical equipment is not sited in such a position that water could increase the hazard associated with it.

Security

Considerations of security might be thought to be only relevant to an investigation into the risks of material damage or of theft of property or information, but it has important implications for the safety of employees. Attempts to steal cash, valuable items or information may present real risks of injury to those employees in whose custody they are, or who are concerned in keeping unauthorised persons from the premises. Politically or socially inspired protest action or attacks on premises may result in injury to those who work there. A properly organised security system must, therefore, include provision for safeguarding people as well as property.

General safety

The risks we have listed so far all bring with them the possibility of injury, but they are not the source of most industrial accidents or disease. Falls, incorrect lifting, and falls of objects are still the most common sources of injury at work. That is to say, most accidents come about as a result of minor inadequacies in the way a company is run. This is not to say that the failures of the system that they represent are unimportant, because many of the major risks that could bring about the collapse of the company may require no greater a failure to produce their catastrophic effects. A review of general safety features in the way in which a company carries on its day-to-day business can be extremely revealing about its general attitude to risk.

Such a review would look at the standard of housekeeping, the layout of the plant, the standard of stairways, floors, roofs and scaffolding and means of access to various parts of the premises. It would consider standards of handling and stacking materials and ways in which internal transport operates. The availability of protective equipment and the extent to which its use is enforced would be checked, as would the general working environment, to ensure that the premises are adequately lit and ventilated, that the dust and noise levels are not excessive, that there is no overcrowding, and that there is no risk from pollutants or radioactivity.

Mechanical and electrical safety

The machinery and plant used would be checked for its safety in operation, and for the effectiveness of guards and other safety devices. Maintenance standards and systems would be examined, and the extent to which spare parts are stocked or available. This could lead on to a consideration of the whole area of contingency planning, which is of importance to the complete risk management programme of a company in enabling it to reduce the period during which its operations could be interrupted.

Electrical safety could also receive attention, to ensure that installations are sound, damaged equipment is not used, that electrical equipment of all kinds is used responsibly, that the necessary stop and isolation switches are supplied, and that there is adequate provision for emergency lighting.

Systems

Apart from the hazards related to the premises and specific items of equipment, the safety review would also consider the basic safety of the systems employed, which in a wider context can give a good indication of the whole approach of the management of a company. Systems of all kinds would be checked, including such things as "permit to work" systems, by which successive stages of a hazardous operation may only be carried out when authorised by a designated person, who is responsible for checking that specified precautions have been taken, and laboratory safety codes. Other considerations would include the general attitude to hygiene throughout the company, the system for ensuring that statutory or other regular examinations of items of plant are carried out, emergency alarm and evacuation systems and the system for training employees, both as newcomers to the company and continuously throughout their service.

Above all, the general system of management control would be studied. This would involve such matters as methods of supervision of employees at work, the importance given to and the nature of accident prevention measures, the role of safety committees and the powers they have to cause action to be taken. The system of reporting accidents and near misses and investigating them to minimise the chance of recurrence of an accident of that type would also be looked at, together with the extent to which employees at all levels are trained in safety, the efficiency of communication in matters of safety and the general reputation of the company, both as an employer and as a neighbour.

A chance to introduce risk management

This list of subjects to be covered in a safety review is far from being exhaustive, but it will be clear from the topics we have mentioned that it will inevitably involve most of the aspects of the way in which the company operates, and it would require the addition of comparatively few other main areas of enquiry for it to become a full risk management audit. The need to comply with health and safety legislation can thus be used as a way of introducing risk management into a company. In many cases, fulfilling the law will involve a review of practices within the company and this can, as we have seen, be extended conveniently to cover other aspects of risk.

Widening views of safety

The concept of health and safety legislation as something entirely internal to a company is in any case breaking down, as general social and environmental concern moves towards seeing the factory not as a world of its own, but as part of the wider environment in which it is situated. It is increasingly becoming recognised that what goes on within the walls of industrial premises may affect the standard of life, or even the life itself, of those who live or work nearby. This trend is emphasised in such legislation as the Health and Safety at Work etc. Act in Britain. The "etc." in the title of the Act is significant, not only because it was the first time the word had been used in the title of legislation, but also because it extends the responsibilities of the employer to include some responsibility towards the public likely to be affected by the way his business is carried on. Health and safety legislation in this case no longer stops at the factory gates, and this widening of the scope of the law should bring with it a trend towards ending the isolation of risks of injury to employees from the other risks which threaten a business.

Increasingly, too, the risk of industrial accidents and disease is moving in its own right into the class of risks which can put a company out of business. The difficulties of coping with the loss brought about by serious industrial diseases which take a long time to develop have been dramatically illustrated by the effects of claims for asbestosis, notably in the USA. There, aided by the steady liberalisation of statutory limitation periods, the flood of claims has overwhelmed asbestos producers, driving some into bankruptcy. Even at a much less dramatic level, failure to provide adequate safety can bring a business to a halt. The Health and Safety at Work etc. Act contains provisions that prohibition notices may be issued by inspectors to prevent any unsafe activity being carried on, or started. We are in the later stages of the transition from a time when it was accepted, for example, that fork grinders would die at about 30, because they ground dry, while table cutlery grinders who ground wet might survive until they were 50, to one where industrial accidents and disease will be considered generally unacceptable. The importance of adequate loss control to prevent them is thus unlikely to diminish; rather it will become an increasingly vital part of a company's total risk management effort.

17. Liability loss control

Special problems of liability threats

The control of legal liabilities is one aspect of loss control that is often overlooked, yet the effects upon a company of a major liability action could be as catastrophic as the destruction of its main premises by fire. Not only could an award these days be of a magnitude which could cause the company serious financial difficulties, but the circumstances in which the liability arose might force it to withdraw its most profitable product from the market, destroy its reputation for service and expertise, or cause it to have to move its manufacturing processes elsewhere.

Much of the neglect of this branch of loss control stems from the fact that a liability is not visible.in the same way that physical disasters are. While it may well be an accident or damage of some kind which produces the liability, the latter is too easily thought of as the concern of the company's lawyers and insurers only. The other main problem in instituting effective liability loss control is that whereas the other major vulnerabilities of a company can be localised, so that the particular process, property, or information can be identified as vitally important and can therefore be protected, liability can be incurred as a result of almost anything that a company does or has done on its behalf, or omits to do or have done. Protection against potential liabilities must therefore be built into the way a company does anything and a protection that has to be so widespread may all too easily be overlooked.

To some extent this problem is eased by the very fact that many liabilities result from injury or damage caused to other people or their property. This means that if systems for the protection of property and people, which we have considered earlier in this book, are effective, then that loss control effort will also act to control the risk of liability. In general, however, this will only hold good for injury or damage caused on or near the company's premises or where the company has some control over the property in question, as may, for example, be the case when it is being transported.

There are, however, two important areas of potential liability which may not be covered by the protection designed to preserve property and people, and which, because of the potential they have for destroying the company or its reputation, call for particular loss control attention. These are the fields of products liability and of professional negligence and we shall look at these in more detail. First of all, however, the general problems posed by the nature of the risk of liability call for closer examination.

In the developed countries, the trend is increasingly towards imposing more and more stringent legal requirements on the way companies do business, particularly in manufacturing industry. As companies have grown larger, there has been an increasing tendency to see any dispute between them and an individual as a "David and Goliath" battle, in which society must help David not only by providing him with ever more accurate slings, but also by holding Goliath still to be hit.

The consumer movement and the growing concern about the quality of life, illustrated by increasing opposition to any form of environmental pollution, have also shaped public feeling about the way in which industry should be permitted to carry on. This has been reflected in the courts, not only by an increase in the potential liabilities of a company (notably if it manufactures products for the general public, when the trend towards strict liability, even perhaps for risks which were not foreseeable when the products were supplied, is marked), but also by increasing awards to those injured or otherwise affected by a failure of a company to comply with standards currently demanded by society. These standards are constantly varying and their trend moves ahead of legislation, so that what is legally permissible may not necessarily be socially acceptable. The control of liability losses cannot therefore be restricted simply to ensuring that the demands of the law are met. It must move further into the field of social risk management to identify those areas of potential loss which, while beyond the limits of legal liability, nevertheless indicate the way that liability, which is ultimately a reflection of the trend of opinion in society, is likely to develop.

Problems associated with liability losses are not limited to those of foreseeing how liability will arise. It is far more difficult to assess the probable severity of a liability loss than one of material damage, or even of loss of earnings. No one can forecast in advance exactly who will be affected by an action of the company, or to what extent they will be affected. Furthermore, the size of a liability incurred may bear no relationship to the importance to the company of the activity which gave rise to it.

Faced with this problem, companies have tended to rely on limitations of liability and on insurance to protect them. In a few cases, statutory limitation of liability is permissible and effective, but elsewhere this method of defence relies on contractual limitations, which are becoming increasingly difficult to enforce in the courts. Many potential claimants will not be in a contractual relationship with the company, so that contract conditions cannot be invoked against them. In other cases, if contractual exclusions of liability are permitted at all, it may well be necessary to demonstrate that not only did the purported limitation cover the exact circumstances in which the claim arose, but also that it was a reasonable limitation and that it was effectively communicated to the claimant in such a way as to make him aware of its existence and terms.

The Unfair Contract Terms Act 1977 prohibits contracting out of liability for death or personal injury resulting from negligence, and makes attempts to contract out of other loss or damage through negligence subject to a test of reasonableness. Where goods are supplied to a consumer, the Act prohibits attempts to contract out of the implied warranty of merchantable quality or fitness for purpose imposed by the Sale of Goods Act 1979. When success in establishing contractual limitation as a defence is seen as such an obstacle course, it cannot be regarded as a satisfactory method of loss control on its own.

The purchase of liability insurance is often less accurately based on the potential size of loss than that of other classes of insurance. To an extent this is understandable since, unlike a material loss, where a value can be assessed for the total loss of the property concerned, the maximum extent of liability cannot be foreseen with any accuracy. A policy limit is often chosen on the basis of premium cost rather than need, ignoring the fact that the company will itself be at risk if the limit chosen should prove to be inadequate. A risk management approach will concentrate insurance buying where it is most needed – at the catastrophic end of the scale – but there may well still be a potentially catastrophic liability exposure for which insurance is not available. Proper loss control is therefore essential.

Products liability

The trend towards strict liability upon a manufacturer for damage or injury caused by his products now seems firmly established in the developed world. Products liability risk control, therefore, can no longer be seen merely in terms of preventing faulty products being released into the market, although this remains a very important aspect of it. Loss control must now include foreseeing possible ways in which products which reach the consumer in exactly the form intended by the manufacturer could result in a liability. This must include considerations of foreseeable incorrect use and possibly even of deliberate misuse. The product itself, its packaging and the instructions which are given about its use, may all be sources of liability and must all be included in the programme of loss control.

The threat of products liability is at its greatest in the United States, but the trend towards strict liability is evident in Europe as well, even though courts' awards are not so alarmingly high on this side of the Atlantic. The EEC Directive on products liability shows that the idea that a product must be faultily manufactured before it can give rise to a liability is far from the case. The Directive defines a defective product as one which "does not provide the safety which a person is entitled to expect, taking all circumstances into account, including the following:

(*a*) the presentation of the product;
(*b*) the use to which it could reasonably be expected that the product would be put;
(*c*) the time when the product was put into circulation."

Preventing the despatch of faulty products calls for good quality control and inspection systems during manufacture, packaging and despatch, but the widening of liability makes it important that loss control should begin before the production stage. Safety has to be designed into the product and thus loss control will also be part of the job of research and development and of designers. It is at this stage that potential liability exposures should be analysed, because if they are recognised at this time, it will be simpler and cheaper to redesign the product to avoid them than if the design has later to be modified during the production stage. If it is left until a complaint or a malfunction reveals the fault, not only may redesign costs be involved, but also the problem and expense of recalling the product from the market; an action which may itself stimulate further claims.

The design should comply with standards or codes of practice or legal requirements which are in force in the countries in which the product is to be distributed and in the countries which border on them, or with which they have regular trading links. Once a product is sold, one cannot forecast exactly where it will be used. It should, of course, be designed to have sufficient resistance to environmental factors and to the conditions to be expected in transport or storage for it not to deteriorate to an unacceptable extent before its expected life in use – in calculating how long that should be, a very liberal margin should be added for contingencies. The design should be considered from the human factors point of view, with the aim of eliminating possible misuse. Similar products already on the market should be studied for the help they can be in building in safety and excluding hazards. This work should continue through production, in the light of information discovered about product performance, using the records of complaints – even if no claims result – as useful indicators of potential hazard. Labelling and instructions for use are also important. Not only must they be complete and explicit, but also they must be in the languages of the countries where use can be foreseen.

Loss control is thus something that involves every stage of the design, manufacturing and selling process and it will also involve such people as a company's customer relations, legal and insurance staff. The way in which enquiries or complaints are handled may have a decisive effect on whether a complaint becomes a liability claim, possibly a very large one, or is an opportunity for the company to convert a present complainant into a future satisfied customer.

Wherever a number of different functions will be taking care of particular aspects of loss control, co-ordination is essential, and this will be one of the key contributions of a central risk management function. It will be particularly important in control of the products liability risk, because of the number of different departments concerned, most of which will report through different chains of organisation and some of which may have very little to do with each other in the normal course of operations.

It is unlikely that it will ever be possible to eliminate the products liability risk entirely, but good liability loss control can reduce the risk substantially. There is always much more scope for preventing a claim than for limiting its size once a cause of action has arisen.

Professional negligence

This may seem, at first sight, to be a risk to which only a few activities are exposed and thus, although it is of extreme importance for them, to be one which need concern most companies very little. The implications of the growing extension of liability for the consequences of advice given or of specialist work performed are, however, of concern to many companies very remote from what might be thought to be "professional" occupations.

There is a growing tendency for a person who gives advice to be responsible for what happens if that advice is taken – the trend is towards presuming that if one purports to have greater knowledge than the layman, one must accept responsibility if following that advice proves to have unfortunate consequences. It is no longer simply those with whom the professional is in a contractual relationship who have a right of action against him. The extent to which an adviser is expected to be right will vary depending on the field in which the advice is given, as will the margin of error allowed to the provider of a specialised professional service. These days, however, if a loss is sustained and professional advice is involved, the temptation to try to recoup the loss by suing the adviser seems to become harder to resist all the time.

What the ordinary manufacturing or distribution company may overlook is the element of professional risk that exists in services provided in support of its business. A design or formulation service may be offered in order to provide a product to meet a customer's specific needs. Technical salesmen may offer, or be called upon to give, advice on suitable applications for a product. The risks involved in these activities can be difficult to identify and even more difficult to control. A desire to help the customer and to increase sales is not an attitude to be discouraged and direct supervision of what is said or offered may in many cases be impossible.

Awareness of the potential risk is a major step towards meeting it, however. Once the possible consequences of a mistaken recommendation or an overenthusiastic claim for performance have been appreciated, loss control becomes very much a matter of education, training and control of personnel. Organisational systems, by which advice or design recommendations are offered in a standard form which can be monitored, can reduce the problem, but ultimately only the people who can create the liability can control the risk. That is the central problem of all liability loss control and one which calls for constant attention in any company.

18. Environmental pollution

Pollution and social risk management

Environmental pollution has, of course, always been a risk, but until comparatively recently its management was largely left to those least equipped to do it – those whose health or enjoyment was affected by it. Now it is increasingly becoming a risk to be managed by the person or organisation that causes it and successful elimination or satisfactory limitation of its effects is fast becoming a condition of carrying on any activity involving actual or potential pollution. "The polluter pays" is now a generally accepted principle for improving the environment and this is backed up by increasingly severe legislation governing environmental conditions both for the workforce and for the public as a whole.

No business concern can, however, rely on simply fulfilling the letter of the law to meet all its obligations in the matter of pollution. Public pressure, reflecting the increased, and increasingly vocal, public concern about the environment, tends to move ahead of legislation. The management of environmental risk thus involves foreseeing the likely trend of public concern, as well as merely complying with current legislation. Social risk management of this kind is not easy to achieve, but intelligent anticipation of future trends is often possible. Action taken to eliminate or reduce the risk before it becomes compulsory can often be easier to put into practice and be more effective than waiting for legislation and having to meet standards imposed by others.

One of the difficulties of managing the risk of pollution lies in the variability of the generally acceptable level of risk. Public opinion, particularly in these days of rapid world-wide communication, can quickly become convinced, either by the activities of pressure groups, or as a response to particular environmental disasters or near-disasters, that a risk which hitherto has been considered acceptable has crossed the boundary into unacceptability. Asbestos, oil and nuclear power are all, in their different ways, examples of the way in which industries have been called upon to design their methods of operation to take account of a substantially increased degree of public concern about them.

Pressure groups are selective in their activity and the occurrence of disaster has a random element about it, so that the progress of compulsory limitation of the pollution risk is not uniform, although general statutes such as the Health and Safety at Work etc. Act 1974 in the United Kingdom lay down overall rules for the way in which industry must take into account the working conditions of its employees and the living conditions of its neighbours in the way it carries on its activities.

It would be unwise, however, for any industry which caused a pollution risk of any kind to assume that because the spotlight of public attention has not yet fallen upon it, it can safely ignore the trend of opinion. If, as sometimes happens, pollution is accepted because of the employment provided by an industry, proper risk management will take into account the possibility of a changed employment situation, which would alter the factors in the equation. Similarly, the next disaster may affect an industry which has so far escaped public notice and bring to the public consciousness a form of pollution not generally known about before. It may be that this pollution is no worse than many others about which the public has not become aware, but protestations about the unfairness of the world are an ineffective risk management tool and something must of course be done about the risk. If they are wise, those other industries whose turn has yet to come will learn from the experience of others and will be doing something about their own environmental risks.

Pollution and changing technology

Throughout his existence Man has modified his environment and the rate at which the adverse effects of the modifications made themselves felt increased as the size of communities became larger. As industrial skills were acquired, so the extent of change necessary to bring about a serious deterioration in the environment grew smaller. Industrial pollution brought about by a change in technology is not a modern phenomenon. Four commissions were set up to investigate the problem of air pollution in London between 1285 and 1310* and it seems probable that the need for them was brought about by a change in technology – in this case the introduction of coal instead of brushwood as a fuel for burning lime for building purposes. The use of coal was banned, but within 20 years the prohibition was forgotten and London faced a pollution problem which lasted over 600 years before the same solution could be re-applied.

The modern risk manager can often learn from history. His problems are often restatements of problems which have faced men many times in the past. An incident such as the above is a reminder that the degree of pollution caused by an industry may not be constant. It may be increased or reduced in amount, or altered in type by any change in technology. The consequences of the variations for risk management should be among

---

*See "Industrial Air Pollution in Thirteenth Century Britain", P. Brimblecombe in *Weather*, Vol. 30 No. 12.

those considered when changes in processes or materials to be used are suggested.

Types of pollution

The forms of pollution which have received most attention in the past have been water and air pollution, but the definition of what constitutes pollution is continually being widened. Pollution of the land is now receiving more attention, while other forms of nuisance are coming to be regarded as "pollution". In this way one speaks of noise pollution or visual pollution and the term is being widened more and more to include anything that detracts from the "quality of life", however that is defined by society at any time. In its widest form, therefore, the management of the risk of pollution extends to include the management of all threats which arise from the physical presence of a company's operations falling short of the standards imposed by the society within which it operates.

Air pollution

In many cases, the major concentration of pollutants will be within the workplace and action to remove them will be necessary to provide a safe working environment. To some extent, therefore, the aims of pollution control will coincide with those of minimising risks to employees. It is, however, no longer acceptable for pollutant-free air in the workplace to be obtained at the expense of increased pollution for the general public in the immediate vicinity. Indeed, concern about pollution is international and on the larger scale it is becoming less acceptable for one country to entrust its pollution to upper air currents for export as acid rain, for example. The emphasis on controlling air pollution will thus increasingly tend to move towards control by engineering and away from reliance on exhaust ventilation, which removes the pollutant from an immediate area and breathing apparatus, which allows work to continue in a polluted atmosphere.

Air pollution can be of several kinds. Some dusts have long been recognised as dangers to health: coal and other silica dusts, cotton, beryllium and others call for special care. The enormous publicity given to the dangers of asbestos fibres in the air both helped to instigate and now reflects serious public concern about a material taken for granted by the man in the street for many years and, ironically, thought of as increasing safety because of its fire-resistant properties. Once there is public disquiet about a material, action must be taken at once to remove the risk of pollution. Vinyl chloride monomer (VCM) and poly-chlorinated biphenyls (PCBs) are examples of hazardous materials, the dangers of which have suddenly come into the public consciousness in this way. Lead levels in the air, notably from the exhausts of motor vehicles, have given rise to more concern as such traffic has increased. Fumes, both from processes involving metals and those involving polymers, cause problems. Certain mists, such as chromic acid mist, can also injure health, while gases may affect respiration, or be toxic irritants, or have narcotic effects.

The main risk management effort will of course be concerned with reducing the concentration of such pollutants where they arise, but care must be taken to ensure that they are not permitted to build up elsewhere to levels which could present a hazard.

Water pollution

There is a growing awareness of the menace of water pollution, whether of inland waters or of the seas, and stringent effluent control is increasingly required. But the more this is insisted upon, the greater will the dependence of many companies be on the continued and efficient working of their effluent treatment plant. In some cases, this may become the key dependency on which the continuance of the earnings from the location hang. Loss control effort must obviously be at its maximum in such circumstances, because a breakdown could mean a double threat to the company: an immediate liability for damage caused by the release of harmful effluent, and a continuing loss of earnings until effluent control measures are once more satisfactory.

Water pollution, basically, assumes one of the following four forms:

(*a*) suspended solids, such as are found in sewage;
(*b*) highly oxidisable organic waste, which is broken down by bacteria;
(*c*) metal and other ions;
(*d*) soluble organic chemicals.

The dimensions of possible disaster arising from water pollution and the public concern about them can be illustrated by two examples of very different kinds of pollution. There was, for instance, the human tragedy caused in Japan to those people whose diet was largely made up of fish which had accumulated high concentrations of mercury as a result of mercury catalyst discharged from a factory producing polyvinyl chloride and acetaldehyde. On the other side of the world, a succession of tanker losses focused attention once again on the possible large-scale damage which may be caused by oil pollution of the seas. The ecological effects of this kind of pollution are unacceptable to a society in which there is increasing concern about the environment, and which is no longer prepared to see the oceans used as convenient dustbins.

Land pollution

To the legacy of the past, in the form of waste heaps, the debris from mines and quarries, industry and the community are still adding pollutants to the ground through the dumping of waste materials. There is, however, mounting concern about the dumping of toxic wastes, and it should clearly form part of the risk management activities of any company which has such wastes to dispose of to satisfy itself that its methods of disposal are safe enough not only to meet present standards, but to comply with possibly more stringent obligations in the future.

The land around a factory may over the years build up excessive levels of contaminants. Instances have been found of high lead content in milk from cattle grazed on land subjected over the years to a "fall-out" from nearby factories. Pollution claims have arisen after many years when what was previously land used for dumping industrial wastes has later been built over. Growing pressures of land use may well combine with the anti-pollution trend in public thinking to make pollution of the land unacceptable.

Other forms of pollution

Noise has increasingly become subject to strict control, as its physiological and psychological effects become more recognised. Here, the best risk management solution is likely to lie in the field of design of machines to limit the noise they emit, rather than in attempts to reduce the intensity or range of the noise produced by external means.

"Pollution" can be extended to include any unwelcome intrusion of man-made activities and the limits of danger to the environment can be drawn so as to include aesthetic as well as material considerations. Risk management in relation to the risk of pollution in this sense must be almost entirely social risk management. It will be based on maintaining an awareness of trends in thought which are likely to affect the general opinion of society, which is ultimately likely to be embodied in legislation. This awareness will be coupled with a continuing realisation that business cannot make its own rules in isolation from the community around it. Avoidance of pollution may eventually become a condition on which business is allowed to operate at all; and since the ultimate aim of risk management is to enable a company to stay in business, a risk of this magnitude must call for particular care in management.

19. Organisation of risk management

Risk management – a job for everyone

The simplicity of the basic principles of risk management and the ease with which it can be broken down into its various stages of risk identification, measurement, control, financing and monitoring can be deceptive. What is easy to describe on paper may be very difficult to introduce into a complex company. Identifying a company's risks may seem a very daunting proposition when these risks are spread out over perhaps hundreds of different locations, when they are linked with and interlinked between many different complicated processes, when the nature of the operations may also be undergoing constant major or minor change.

If one sets the theory of risk management against such a background – the background it must have if it is translated from the textbook into real life – it immediately becomes apparent that it is not a one-man job. No one man is likely to have the range of knowledge and skills necessary to undertake the management of the whole of a company's vast range of risk himself. Even if such a polymath could be found, he might well have difficulty in communicating his ideas to all the many managers, all busy with their own problems, and in persuading them that risk management was something they should be aware of and care about. Indeed, if a superman of a "risk manager" is going to manage the risk, why should they bother?

As has been pointed out in discussing its various stages, risk management must therefore be a job for everyone in the company. No company, however, will reach a state where risk management is generally accepted and practised unless there is some conscious introduction of its principles. Such an introduction can only be inspired from the top of the company. Proclaimed anywhere else in the organisation, risk management could easily be viewed as merely a piece of empire building by its sponsors, and it runs the risk of being too narrowly defined in terms of the particular specialisation of those introducing it.

The risk management policy statement

The key to the successful introduction of risk management lies in the commitment of top management to its principles and it is a sound beginning if that commitment is expressed in the form of a policy statement issued by the Board. This should set out clearly what risk management is and the benefits which its introduction should bring to the company. It should go on to spell out the responsibility of each line manager in the company to support the policy and to manage risk within his own area of authority. If this is not done, managers may well approve of the introduction of risk management as an idea, but leave its implementation to others.

In practice, one finds that surprisingly few companies have drawn up such a policy statement. Those that have done so are largely the type of company which has a strongly centralised organisation and which makes great use of procedural manuals. A risk management policy statement easily finds a place in such a manual, where it will usually be associated with loss control or insurance buying activities.

It is, however, decentralised companies which probably have the greatest need for a clear statement of company policy. Without such guidance, standards of risk management may fluctuate widely and dangerously from one part of the company to another, as each local manager takes his own view of its importance.

Emphasis on the responsibility of everyone to manage risk becomes particularly important if the issue of the policy statement coincides with the appointment of a "risk manager" as part of the general measures to introduce risk management into the company. This is, perhaps, an unfortunate choice of job title, for what, one might think, is the job of a "risk manager" if not to manage risk? It is far better and far more descriptive of his real function in the company to describe him as a risk management adviser, for he is there to advise, help, persuade and encourage others to manage the risks of their particular part of the company, not to manage the company's risks himself.

A statement that it is the responsibility of all to manage risk will achieve little on its own. The policy must be enforced by writing accountability for risk management performance into job descriptions. In most companies it will be necessary for this accountability to be expressed in the same terms as others, such as a financial budget, or a target to be met. This in turn will mean that there must be a mechanism for the direct and indirect costs of loss to be included as a factor in reviewing management performance, since they represent risk not managed.

The risk manager's function

Obviously managers will need advice, help and training in the management of risk and this will be the key task of the risk management adviser. In some company structures, it will not be possible for the risk manager (if, for the sake of convenience, we can use the term in common use, despite its misleading nature) to have a purely advisory role and he will be expected to take on some specific executive functions. Most commonly these will be in the field of risk financing, with the placing of insurance and the management of self-insurance schemes as the most important features. These are functions which are most efficient when centralised and it is reasonable that they should come within a risk manager's scope. Most of today's risk managers, however, are former insurance managers and the temptation must be there for them to see risk financing as their real job and to relegate the advisory side of their work to a secondary place.

Insurance men are not alone in this tendency to give the specialist part precedence over the general. It is as easy for risk management to be seen as mainly fire prevention or mainly industrial health and safety, for example, if a specialist in those fields becomes the risk manager. To counteract this tendency the risk manager's job specification should emphasise the essentially advisory nature of the work. It is not enough to define the risk manager's role so that he understands it himself. His function must be publicised throughout the company, so that line managers know that his help is available to them and also that they will be expected to make use of that help. Once again, the importance of top management backing for the introduction of risk management can be seen to be essential for its success.

Company style

The other prerequisite for effective risk management is that it should be introduced in a way that fits in with the individual "company style" of the organisation. Risk management should be introduced as part of the overall way in which a company is managed and it is therefore unrealistic to expect it to be successful if it requires a style of action or of thinking unrelated to other aspects of management in the company.

The aims of risk management must be set out in the policy statement in terms which reflect the company's approach. If it seeks to emphasise its social responsibility, then risk management should be interpreted in those terms; if it is essentially profit-orientated, then the financial contribution risk management will make through reducing costs can be stressed.

Similarly, the way in which risk management is organised must be in keeping with the company style. If the company is decentralised, then risk management must also be decentralised. A central risk management department seeking to influence the way in which day-to-day risk management should be carried on in otherwise autonomous divisions or subsidiary companies would be unlikely to have any success. Much more probably, it would be seen as an interfering arm of central management, to be viewed with extreme suspicion and given as little co-operation as possible. In such a company, it will probably be more effective to establish a number of separate decentralised risk management advisory functions. A central risk manager will still be needed, but his function may very well be that of a co-ordinator of co-ordinators.

A multinational company will inevitably be decentralised to some extent and the differences in social, economic and business conditions between one country and another will affect risk management as much as any other management function. The broad aims of risk management will of course be the same wherever the company operates, but the way they are achieved may very well have to vary from place to place, adopting a local accent and style in each.

Problems in introducing risk management

No change as far-reaching as the introduction of organised risk management into a company can be expected to be free of problems. Line managers may be required to manage their own risks, but risk does not come in neat, departmentalised packages. It spills across functional and organisational boundaries, so that one risk will involve a number of functions which may have different reporting channels. Co-ordination will therefore be necessary and it is here that a central risk management adviser can be useful. If he is to work effectively, however, he needs good communications, both formal and informal, with all who are directly concerned in identifying and dealing with risk. Such communication may cut across established chains of command and carries with it the risk that the risk manager may be suspected of being an information-gathering spy for the section of central management to which he reports.

Risk management in an organised form may be a new thing for the company, but many of its constituent parts will have existed in the company already. The company may well have long established fire prevention specialists, safety officers, security men, quality control departments, customer relations officers, legal advisers or insurance departments, all of which can be said to be engaged in partial risk management. It is improbable that they will be working together in any organised way – or the company would be well on the way to practising risk management already. More usually they will only have any contact when their specialisations come into conflict, as with the common clash between the man whose concern is with the security of the premises and the one who is seeking to ensure safe means of escape from them in an emergency.

The introduction into the company of a risk manager who seeks to dictate how each of these separate specialist domains is to be managed is likely to lead to more resentment than co-operation. The solution to his problem, as to that of company-wide direct communication, will lie in a clear definition of the risk manager's function and in an emphasis on his role as a co-ordinator in those areas where risk is already managed and an adviser on risk management techniques where it is not.

There will usually be some psychological problems involved in introducing risk management, which only the risk management adviser himself can solve. Essentially, risk management requires people to consider the possibility of things going wrong in their own sphere of activity, and that is something that few of us like doing, despite the *Schadenfreude* which can make the contemplation of other people's potential disasters a pleasant pastime. Interruption of our normal activities is something most of us would prefer just not to think about. Alternatively, the prospect may leave people unconcerned, either because they are too optimistic about their ability to keep going by improvisation when disaster strikes or because, on the other hand, they are too pessimistic about the chances of doing anything about it. "If it happens", they think, "it happens and that's that." These attitudes lead to inertia and risk management will have to be presented to these people in terms which show either the need for, or the possibility of, risk control. In either case, persuasiveness will be a useful characteristic for the risk manager to have.

Suggesting that things may go wrong can be even more difficult if one is dealing with one of the company's technical experts. He may see his job largely as ensuring that things do not go wrong and may take a suggestion that disaster is possible as casting doubts on his professional competence. The fact that risk management is the co-ordination of well-tried techniques rather than an entirely new one may not help. If risk management is presented in the company as something new and different, yet appears to the specialist to consist of applying procedures he already knows about under another name, the impression of an outsider trying to teach him his job may be strengthened and professional pride prove an even greater barrier to overall risk management. Diplomacy will clearly be another quality of the successful risk manager.

The risk manager's place in the company structure

Just as the "company style" will determine the way in which risk management is practised within a company, so it should decide where the risk management function should appear in the company's organisation chart. Many companies include it as part of the central financial function, on the grounds that the effects of risk ultimately affect the company in financial terms. Other companies, who put the emphasis on the loss control aspects of risk management and whose approach to it may have been from safety or loss prevention rather than insurance, may see the risk management function as part of technical management.

Neither of these areas has any sort of prescriptive right to direct risk management in a company. The central risk management adviser may be located anywhere that suits the company, although to be effective he needs to have access to top management in order to obtain the backing he needs to introduce a co-ordinated pattern of risk management. He also needs good communications with all parts of the organisation, and this is often easier if his reporting lines emphasise staff rather than line functions. He needs to be like a spider, with his company as the web. He can be anywhere in it, but his communications should be such that if risk touches the web at any point, the vibrations will reach him at once and he can be quickly on hand to deal with it. But he will not, and cannot, deal with it alone – risk management is a co-operative effort involving everyone, and the correct risk management organisation for any company is the one that enables and encourages that effort to deal with its own particular risks to be most effective.

20. The future of risk

Static and dynamic risks

If we could know the future, there would be no risk and hence no need for risk management. In our perpetual state of uncertainty we must make the best guesses possible about what the future will hold and always be ready to modify our ideas in the light of events. This pattern applies to all human activity. Risk management sets out to provide an ordered way of making those guesses about the threats to the assets and earnings of a company, and of making plans to counter them based on those guesses. In this way it seeks to increase the confidence a company can have in its ability to attain its corporate goals. The risk manager's work thus parallels that of the corporate planner – the latter charts where the company aims to be in the future, while the former tries to identify and eliminate the hindrances which may prevent it from reaching that goal.

These potential hindrances can be divided into two broad categories. The first, which have been called "static risks", comprises those threats which are always with us and present the same essential problems at all times, although they may manifest their specific effects in countless different ways. The perils of nature are an example of this type of risk, as is the propensity of human beings to error and the warlike side of their nature. The second category consists of what have been called "dynamic risks" which change as society changes. Social and political risks of all kinds will, of course, be included in it. So will such man-made risks as that of legal liability. It will extend to include technological and social developments which influence either the probability or the potential severity of the constant risks.

The changing emphasis in risk

For most of Man's history, it has been the static risks which have presented the greatest threat to him and to his business, since it is only in fairly recent times that business and life can be really distinguished. Fire, storm, sickness and the destruction of war held most terror for pre-industrial man. With the coming of the industrialised society, the basic pattern did not change very much. The scale of possible disaster became greater – a dynamic risk affected the pattern to that extent – but the same perils were the chief threats to business.

In today's society, however, we can detect a clear trend towards dynamic risks becoming the major problem and the indication is that this trend will continue. It used to be generally possible to assume that for a manufacturing company at least, fire at its main production premises was the most serious external risk it faced. Ask many companies now where the potential disaster lies and the answer will not be in fire, but in products liability. The static risk is overshadowed by the dynamic one.

The static risk does not vanish, of course – it will always be with us – and, indeed, its likelihood and the extent of the damage that it could cause are increasing all the time because of the dynamic risks that affect it. The growing size of industrial units and their concentration have put much larger sums at risk at one time and the reduction in the number of suppliers of many materials has meant that the effects of a loss will be wider-ranging than was once the case. The flexibility that industry once had in the methods and the raw materials it used and in the markets it served has frequently been diminished. Large capacity plants designed for a single type of raw material and depending on a very high utilisation for profitability have not only increased the amounts at risk, but at the same time have reduced the company's ability to improvise after a loss to maintain some production and so to diminish its effects.

Industry, the community and risk

Concerned public opinion, following some spectacular individual disasters, is much less happy about the size and concentration of industrial plants. Major hazards legislation now seeks to control the quantities of hazardous materials handled or stored, again as a result of pressure from those who see industry as imposing unacceptable risks upon its neighbours, risks which were the more unacceptable for being, in many cases, undisclosed. Both these trends reflect the increasing involvement of the community in industry which tends to work in favour of a reduction of certain kinds of risk. Even in industrial recession, when the community might be expected to accept industry on any terms because of the importance of the employment it provides, the heightened awareness of the risks it presents still operates to put constraints on what is acceptable. The same can be said of agitation about pollution of all kinds and the conservation of resources. But, while such community interest tends to diminish some risks, it puts new ones in their place. The increasing risk of incurring liability, which has already been mentioned, is one of the effects on industry of greater public involvement in determining how, and to what standards, it is to operate.

A few years ago, concern was being expressed about the rapidly increasing rate of change, both social and technological, which threatened to overwhelm Man's powers of adaptation. There are signs of a desire to put the brakes on at least some of these aspects of change. Technological innovation in the industries which have been the chief centres of interest for growing social concern, such as pharmaceuticals, are finding the rewards of innovation diminishing as the amount of evidence of safety of new products that has to be produced to regulatory authorities and the liability risks inherent in failure increase. Some even see in this the start of a decline in the spirit of scientific enquiry and its replacement by a risk-averse caution. This trend, however, is neither sufficiently strong nor sufficiently widespread for us to be able to discard altogether the idea of increasing change as one of the major factors in our future uncertainty.

Risk management in the future

What is clear is that the days when a company and its risks were its own affair are gone. It is part of the community and the community will increasingly demand a say in how it is managed. The consumer will decide more and more what is to be produced, society will control ever more rigorously how it shall be manufactured, and employees will participate more and more in the company's management. Risk management then will become more and more obviously a matter of charting a path for a company which avoids it getting so far out of line with what these various forces require of it that it incurs crippling penalties, whether in the form of compensation for a legal liability, or of being prevented from operating in some way.

The danger is, of course, that risk management may then be seen to be almost exclusively concerned with dynamic risks of this kind and neglect what is now its main preoccupation – the static risks. This could be a victory for the wider view of risk management that this book has advocated, but it would be a victory gained at a potentially disastrous price. For the static risks never go away. Fire will still destroy, human factors will still contrive to outwit the most complicated safety systems and, even if technological development and industrial concentration go no further than the point they have reached today, the consequences may still be catastrophic. The rate of change may not prove as headlong in the future as has been feared, but it is still certain that there will be change. That a thing is possible has always been Man's justification for doing it and curiosity, though it may be made more difficult to exercise, can never be switched off altogether. Conventional defences against the age-old perils must therefore continue to be improved, with better and more effective systems designed to prevent the risk materialising, and to minimise its effects if it cannot be prevented.

Risk management is as much concerned with the threats everyone recognises as with those that require careful investigation and this is unlikely to change in the future. There may be a danger, however, that, because the management of dynamic risks requires a constantly changing strategy, and possibly a much more sophisticated risk identification technique, it could become such a fascinating and absorbing exercise that the more mundane battle against the static risks could be forgotten.

Alternatively, because it is essentially always the same battle, it might be delegated to a specialist fairly low down in the company hierarchy. If this were to happen, then the development of risk management would really be back where it started. The old-style insurance manager, with his concern for a narrow range of specific threats, would effectively have been re-invented, responsibility for managing risk would be split, there would be a tendency for management of static risks to be left to the specialist and the important effect dynamic risks can have on the way the static risks manifest themselves could easily be ignored as falling between the two specialisations.

All this is, of course, speculation. Risk management still has a long way to develop before it could decline in this way. A more likely danger is that it will not develop sufficiently in many companies before the increasing confusion and interdependence of so-called "commercial", "insurable", "political" and "social" risk become so great that they overwhelm any attempt to manage them by the old method of separate and independent specialisations.

This very confusion shows risk for what it is – a single, many-faceted entity, which needs co-ordinated management. And since it affects every aspect of the company's operations and every person in it, everyone must be involved in it. If threats to a company are increasingly likely to present themselves as a composite of different kinds of risk, then an overall method of dealing with them as a whole will be essential. It may be an interesting academic exercise to analyse the compound risk into its component parts and to label each, but to do so with the object of parcelling out the responsibility for managing each part to a separate person or department is to create an internal risk potentially as serious as any of the external ones.

When it looks into the future, a company can be sure that it will be faced with risk, but it can never know the exact form of that risk. If its management of risk is too closely tied to specialist solutions to particular types of risk problems, then, as risks become greater both in size and in complexity, so the chances increase of a risk problem arising for which no solution, or no system for finding a solution, has been provided. If, on the other hand, risk management is seen as a part of the general management process and tackles risk as a whole, then the system will be flexible enough to adapt to whatever the shape that future threats to its existence may take. Risk management, as we have tried to show, is more than a set of individual tactics. It should be an overall strategy designed to give a company the basic security of knowing that it can stay in business.

Index

Index